ETHICS, RELIGION AND BIODIVERSITY

ETHICS, RELIGION AND BIODIVERSITY

RELATIONS BETWEEN CONSERVATION AND CULTURAL VALUES

edited by

Lawrence S. Hamilton

Program on Environment, East-West Center

with the assistance of

Helen F. Takeuchi

The White Horse Press

CONTENTS

FIGURES AND TABLES

FIGURES

TABLES

ETHICS, RELIGION AND BIODIVERSITY

PREFACE

The papers herein were presented at a symposium in the XVII Pacific Science Congress held in Honolulu, Hawai'i, from May 27 to June 2, 1991. This symposium was organized by a forest biologist who long ago recognized that the application of more ecological science alone will not halt the serious loss of genes, species, and ecosystems; nor will recycling of aluminum or application of more pollution control technology do the trick. These tools and methods reduce the magnitude of environmental degradation, but they do not get at the cause of the problem. The same is true for economic manipulations in favor of conservation, even though the emerging field of ecological-economics is a promising and long overdue development. In my lecturing days at Cornell University in the seventies I used to say: "It is not the ecologists, engineers, economists, or earth scientists who will save spaceship earth, but the poets, priests, artists, and philosophers." I obviously still believe that assertion, which resulted in this symposium in the Pacific Science Congress. The symposium focused on ethics, values, and religions as bases for biological diversity conservation – one very key part of caring for the planet and reducing its rate of impoverishment.

My first concrete and dramatic personal encounter with biodiversity conservation through religious taboo came in Venezuela in the early seventies. I was engaged in a study of tropical rainforest use and preservation in that country. Landless or land-hungry campesinos were nibbling away at the retreating edges of most reserved forest areas. One substantial area surrounded by converted land remained largely unaffected. This was the forest of the goddess María Lionza who rode a tapir and who reputedly dealt harshly with anyone who destroyed her forest abode. I learned that the cult of María Lionza persisted, and was held to, even by many urbanites in Caracas.

The Monumento Natural de María Lionza of some 40,000 hectares at that time was the most protected area of rainforest in all of Venezuela, and still is today, I am sure. I began at that point to collect material on forests that were afforded a measure of protection by religious awe, reverence, or fear. One of the most interesting examples occurs in Yunnan, China, in the prefecture of Xishuangbanna. According to Pei (Chapter 6), forests of the holy hills in the region are protected as the abode of the ancestors' spirits by the *Dai* people. These protected forests constitute about 2 percent of the prefecture's land area.

In the major Congress theme of Biological Diversity, this rather unusual mini-symposium addressed nonbiological aspects which undergird and are necessary for any change in the world's attitude toward biodiversity conservation. Let us speak then to natural scientists and others about these intangible and often "uncomfortable" (for many of us) topics which many regard as "soft." We are now in good company. An "Appeal for Joint Commitment in Science and Religion" was presented in Moscow in January 1990 at the Global Forum of Spiritual and Parliamentary Leaders. It was organized by Dr. Carl Sagan and signed by 32 world-renowned scientists including Stephen Jay Gould, Gyorgi Galitsyn, Sir Frederick Warner, Hans Bethe, Mohammed Kassas, and James Hansen. The appeal stated in part, after listing some of the more serious "Crimes Against Creation":

> By their very nature these assaults on the environment were not caused by any one political group or any one generation. Intrinsically, they are transnational, transgenerational and transideological. So are all conceivable solutions. To escape these traps requires a perspective that embraces all the peoples of the planet and all the generations yet to come.

> Problems of such magnitude, and solutions demanding so broad a perspective must be recognized from the outset as having a religious as well as a scientific dimension. Mindful of our common responsibility, we scientists – many of us long engaged in combating the environmental crisis – urgently appeal to the world religious community to commit, in word and deed, and as boldly as is required, to preserve the environment of the Earth.

Three hundred and seventy spiritual leaders from 83 countries – Patriarchs, Lamas, Chief Rabbis, Grand Muftis, Archbishops, Cardinals, and Mullas – endorsed this appeal. More recently, late in 1992, over 1,600 scientists, including 101 Nobel Prize winners, signed a "global warning" calling for a new ethic – a new attitude toward caring for ourselves and for the earth.

The Dalai Lama has enunciated a proposal for combining nature protection with opportunity for liberation of the human spirit. He proposed that Tibet be transformed into a peace sanctuary and "creative zone" where traditional Tibetan culture, wild flora and fauna, and human activity could coexist in a Zone of Ahisma or nonviolence.

One of the authors (Engel) in this volume is currently working with scientists in the World Conservation Union (IUCN) to bring the ethical and religious elements into the Global Biodiversity Strategy. His presentation gives an action blueprint.

But, it is not the scientific community in general that needs a basic change in values and attitudes about nature. Many scientists indeed have experienced profound stirrings of awe and reverence as they explore the natural and physical world and universe.

It is a heedless consumer-culture (particularly in the developed world) and the unmitigated faith in the ability of science and technology to provide ever-increasing levels of consumption and supposed "welfare" that needs to be changed in relationship with the Earth. Science and technology can be useful means of reducing the rate of environmental degradation; but the roots of the matter have to do with stewardship, equity, justice, and the inherent worth of living things. Ethics, values, and religions are keys to the necessary altered attitudes and behaviors. Therefore, in this volume we hope to present insights into our relationship with both the natural and human modified worlds as we focus on how these beliefs and behaviors affect biological diversity conservation.

We cannot assure the conservation of biological diversity by setting aside a few national parks and protected areas, even in a global system representative of the Earth's major biogeographical zones. We can only conserve most of the wonderful wealth of genes, species, and communities by a stewardship which is part of the fabric of human society and culture. This has been the situation (and to some extent still is) with livelihood in many traditional religions and value systems. A few of these are documented in chapters in this volume. It is apparent, however, that many of these conserving values and beliefs are eroding, and the challenge is one of the development of new ethics toward nature, and to the concept of biodiversity conservation. This volume sets forth material which should improve our understanding of the biophysical-metaphysical interactions and aid us in meeting this challenge.

Lawrence S. Hamilton
Program on Environment
East-West Center

INTRODUCTION

Lawrence S. Hamilton

OUR BIODIVERSITY WEALTH

We put our monetary wealth in safes, in banks with guards, or even in fortresses to prevent theft. We often protect our cultural treasures in museums, again with guards. Yet we allow our wonderful biological wealth to be pilfered or destroyed with little concern. Although almost 7,000 areas have been categorized as parks and nature reserves, which have been designated for protection and conservation of biological diversity, they are less than 5 percent of the Earth's land surface and a minuscule portion of the marine environment. Moreover, these areas are faced with increasing assault under pressures of land hunger or "development." Parks and reserves alone will not conserve our biological heritage. Areas where humans work, play, forage, and worship are cultural landscapes and seascapes, and have key roles to play also.

The amazing and valuable biological diversity of the Earth, essential for human life support, consists of genes, species, and ecosystems in all their exuberant variety. *Genetic diversity* is the variation among genes within species. This diversity not only gives rise to distinct populations of the same species (e.g., the thousands of local rice varieties in India), but it also accounts for variation within a population where, for example, one individual may have more disease resistance than another. *Species diversity* is the variety of species in a given geographic area. For the entire planet, there is wondrous abundance. For example, about 10 million (between 5 and 20 million) species exist. Of these, 50 to 90 percent are found in tropical forests (WRI, IUCN, UNEP 1992). Great species diversity can be found in relatively small areas; for instance, there may be as many as 150 species of trees alone on 1 hectare of tropical rainforest. In the Hawaiian Islands at the time of Captain James Cook's arrival in 1778, there were probably 1,200 to 1,300 species of native flowering plants, about 90 percent of which were not found anywhere else in the world (called endemics) (Sohmer and Gustafson 1987). *Ecosystem diversity* is the variety of associations of species and their interacting physical environment. These can be identified at various scales at local, regional, national, or global levels. A small Pacific island at a gross scale might have the following natural ecosystems: upland rainforests, leeward dry forests, freshwater swamps, mangrove forests, coastal strands, beaches, streams, coral reefs, seagrass beds, and marine near-shore environments.

The global storehouse of living matter is vast, but it is being impoverished by human actions in a reckless, spendthrift way that can lead only to bankruptcy. The loss is occurring at all three levels of biological diversity. At the genetic level, 1,500 local rice varieties have become extinct in the past 15 years in Indonesia alone (WRI, IUCN, UNEP 1992). In Hawai'i, at least 10 percent of the native plant species is now believed to be extinct, and 30 percent of the remainder is considered endangered or threatened. Birds of Hawai'i have suffered even greater destruction with 24 of the 71 endemics extinct and 28 species on the endangered list (Hawai'i Audubon Society 1989). Tropical forests, which host between 50 and 90 percent of the total world species, are disappearing through clearing at an annual rate of 17 million hectares (an area four times the size of Switzerland) (FAO 1990). The loss of biological diversity is alarming. E. O. Wilson (1980) puts it succinctly and forcibly:

> The worst thing that can happen – will happen in the 1980s – is not energy depletion, economic collapse, limited nuclear war, or conquest by a totalitarian government. As terrible as these catastrophes would be for us, they can be repaired within a few generations. The

one process ongoing in the 1980s that will take millions of years to correct is the loss of genetic and species diversity by the destruction of natural habitats. This is the folly our descendants are least likely to forgive us.

MAIN MECHANISMS OF BIODIVERSITY LOSS

Genes, species, and ecosystems are not static in the natural world. Natural disasters such as volcanic eruptions, competition in changing environments due to climatic change, and other cataclysmic events have characterized the long progression of life on this planet, and have been responsible for biodiversity loss, acting as a countervailing force in the evolution of new biological diversity. But technological advances have been responsible for an unprecedented increase in extinctions, and the rate of loss is increasing. Some scientists believe that about 25 percent of the world's species could be lost over the next three decades from tropical forests alone, if the present rate of forest destruction continues (Raven 1988).

The loss of natural ecosystems as they are converted to farms, ranches, mines, reservoirs, and cities, or fragmented into nonviable patches by these conversions or by the infrastructures that are associated with them, reduces the habitat for species and their genetic variability. This is a major mechanism for biodiversity reduction.

The contamination of ecosystems may not only be toxic to plants and animals but may disrupt the functioning of ecosystem processes, thereby contributing to loss and impairing the human life-support systems. Soil contamination and freshwater pollution from pesticides, overfertilization, and chemical wastes have resulted in death of or stress on many avian, terrestrial, and aquatic species. At sea, oil spills, toxic waste dumping, and radioactive waste disposal have taken their toll. Forest removal and faulty irrigation have rendered millions of hectares of land so saline that neither crops nor former vegetation will grow. Air pollution has heavily damaged forest and freshwater lake ecosystems in North America, Europe, and some of the former Soviet republics.

Alien plant and animal introductions have had a devastating effect on native biological diversity, especially on small oceanic islands where flora and fauna developed in isolation from persistent invasion pressures from predators, competitors, and pests. It has been human introduction of alien species that has been responsible for most of the species loss and endangerment in Hawai'i. Even larger islands such as New Zealand and the continent of Australia have adversely impacted their biodiversity through deliberate and accidental introductions over the past 200 years since European contact.

Commercial (industrial-type) agriculture and forestry have been based on developing simple, even monocultural, systems to replace the complex species richness of the natural vegetation. Species, ecosystems, and valuable genes have been lost in this process. Traditional agriculturists and graziers maintained great genetic variation and species variation also, as a risk minimization strategy. Moreover, because different races or varieties of a species had different flavor, time of ripening, disease resistance or other characteristics desirable for subsistence, this variation was enhanced by breeding. Mixing species spatially or sequentially gave variety in diet, reduced pest damage, and often resulted in better use of the natural productivity of the site. The spread of commercial "big" agriculture and grazing has led to an emphasis on only a few species, and on a constrained genetic make-up of bred varieties. Of the 75,000 plants known to be edible, we rely on only 20 for 90 percent of our food (WWF 1986). Industrial forestry, too, has in the past converted native complex forests to single- or few-species plantations, usually alien introductions that grow rapidly. Although some of the germplasm for the more important agricultural and forestry crops has been stored in gene banks, many varieties have been lost, and storage is not without seed deterioration problems to compound the loss.

Overharvesting of wild species as in fishing, logging, hunting or trapping, and collecting (gathering) is seldom enough of a pressure to eliminate a species by itself, but when coupled with any of the other mechanisms, such pressure can lead to reduced abundance, threatened status, and even to extinction. High technology, a very efficient means of exploitation, has given humans awesome power in this respect. Driftnets are not only severely depleting target stocks of fish, but adversely impacting nontarget organisms such as dolphins. Although clearing forest habitat was the major pressure that caused extinction of the once super-abundant passenger pigeon, the slaughter, in which freight cars full of birds were transported to markets, was certainly of compelling force also.

Industrialized humankind has caused a measurable increase in "greenhouse gases," particularly carbon dioxide and methane, and in compounds that reduce the protective ozone layer. The probable global warming, the possible associated sea level rise, and the increase in ultraviolet light reaching the Earth's surface will have profound effects on all living things. If the effects are rapid, species and communities may not be able to change or migrate fast enough to maintain a place in the biodiversity treasure house. Under a scenario of rapid climate change, mountain ecosystems will be the most seriously affected; and if there is a rise in sea level, coastal ecosystems and atolls will be drastically altered or eliminated.

CONSERVATION OF BIOLOGICAL DIVERSITY

In the search for solutions to the crisis of rapidly declining biodiversity scientific research, technology and economics are of great importance. We urgently need more information about ecosystems, species, and genes: how many? what condition? and where? We have identified and catalogued only a small fraction (perhaps 14 percent) of the world's species. Costa Rica has recently established a National Biodiversity Institute (INBIO) and is attempting the Herculean task of a complete species inventory and data bank in 10 years. Certainly also, changed technology can help to reduce the impacts of some of the mechanisms causing biodiversity loss just enumerated. This is particularly true in terms of reducing or eliminating pollution and reducing the anthropogenic causes of climate change. "Rescue" in botanical and zoological gardens and gene bank storage are warranted. Breeding and genetic research may assist in saving and even reconstituting some of the genetic variation. Better economic valuation of what biodiversity means to societies and to economies may help inform the public that the costs of conservation are offset by financial benefits. Some of the financial arguments that have been advanced are indeed impressive. For instance, economic benefits from wild species are worth $87 billion annually in the United States alone; traditional plant and animal medicines from wild species are the basis for health care for about 80 percent of the people in developing countries; even in the United States, one-fourth of all prescription drugs dispensed contain active ingredients from plants and more than 3,000 antibiotics are derived from micro-organisms (WRI, IUCN, UNEP 1992).

However, in the last analysis, it is true that the scientific, technological, or economic solutions even in concert cannot do the job, because they will not be applied in a timely manner or sufficient in thoroughness unless humankind commits itself to a moral imperative to conserve life. "No survival without a world ethic," says Hans Küng, Director of the Institute for Ecumenical Research at the University of Tübingen, Germany (Küng 1991). Science, technology, and more inclusive economics can be useful means of reducing the rate of environmental degradation and concomitant loss of biodiversity. They may help us to shape an ecologically sustainable type of development. But the roots of the matter have to do with stewardship, equity, justice, and the inherent worth of living things. Ethics, cultural values, and religions are keys to the necessary altered attitudes and behaviors. Thomas Berry, Director of the Riverdale Center for Religious Research in New York, puts it this way: "Our most basic obligation is to honor the earth that brought us forth and to sustain, so far as we are able, those same creative activities that brought forth the mountains and rivers and valleys, the forests, the plains, the blossoming flowers, the singing birds, the turtles and fish in the sea, and indeed all those constituent members of our earthly community" (Berry 1992). In 1991, the World Conservation Union proposed a strategy for sustainable living called *Caring for the Earth*. A statement from their book is reproduced below as Elements of a World Ethic for Living Sustainably (IUCN, UNEP, WWF 1991).

Every human being is part of the community of life, made up of all living creatures. This community links all human societies, present and future generations, and humanity and the rest of nature. It embraces both cultural and natural diversity.

Every human being has the same fundamental and equal rights, including: the right to life, liberty, and security of person; to the freedoms of thought, conscience, and religion; to enquiry and expression; to peaceful assembly and association; to participation in government; to education; and, within the limits of the Earth, to the resources needed for a decent standard of living. No individual, community, or nation has the right to deprive another of its means of subsistence.

Each person and each society is entitled to respect of these rights and is responsible for the protection of these rights for all others.

Every life form warrants respect independently of its worth to people. Human development should not threaten the integrity of nature or the survival of other species. People should treat all creatures decently and protect them from cruelty, avoidable suffering, and unnecessary killing.

Everyone should take responsibility for his or her impacts on nature. Peoples should conserve ecological processes and the diversity of nature, and use any resource frugally and efficiently, ensuring that their uses of renewable resources are sustainable.

Everyone should aim to share fairly the benefits and costs of resource use among different communities and interest groups, between present and future generations. Each generation should leave to the future a world that is at least as diverse and productive as the one it inherited. Development of one society or generation should not limit the opportunities of other societies or generations.

The protection of human rights and those of the rest of nature is a worldwide responsibility that transcends all cultural, ideological, and geographical boundaries. The responsibility is both individual and collective.

HOPEFUL INDICATORS

Action is afoot! From many directions we hear of new awareness of
the need for moral recognition of responsibility to all creatures on this
Earth. *Caring for the Earth* is one of a growing number of actions.
Organized religions are joining forces to promote an earth ethic
among their adherents. Progress in this movement was reported eight
times a year in a journal called *The New Road,* which was produced
from 1986 till 1992 by the World Wide Fund for Nature in Gland,
Switzerland. Representatives of some 50 religious communities gathered recently in Geneva to draft a common proposal calling for respect
of order in the universe and a new relationship between humans and
nature. This was transmitted to the Earth Summit in Río de Janeiro in
June 1992 as a contribution to the Earth Charter. A complex series of
negotiations by an intergovernmental committee and scientific advi-
sors resulted in a Convention on Biological Diversity, which was
subscribed to at the Earth Summit by 153 nations. One of the authors
of a chapter in this book has been instrumental in shaping the ethical
dimensions of the World Conservation Union position, and two other
authors have been working on the U.S. government's policies with
respect to environmental ethics and ethical development. In the
preface to this book, the 1990 Moscow "Global Forum of Spiritual and
Parliamentary Leaders" was mentioned, where 370 spiritual leaders
from 83 countries endorsed an "Appeal for Joint Commitment in
Science and Religion" authored by 32 world-renowned scientists to
redress crimes against creation.

The number of natural or near-natural areas set aside largely for
nature conservation in parks and other reserves continues to increase
steadily despite the tremendous pressures for unbridled economic
development in all parts of the globe. There are now around 7,000
areas covering over 650 million hectares. In February 1992, approximately 1,600 parks people gathered in Caracas, Venezuela, at the IV
World Parks Congress to hear heartening results since the last Congress 10 years previously. In that time period, 1,779 sites covering

nearly 142 million hectares had been designated. They laid out a blueprint for the next 10 years under the theme "Parks for Life."

Courses dealing with environmental ethics are being taught in major universities in the United States. Major books have been written over the past few years with such titles as *Environmental Ethics, Ethics of Environment and Development, The Greening of the Church,* and *Global Responsibility: In Search of a New World Ethic.* They are bringing a disturbing but exciting message to thousands. We hope this present book is also a significant contribution to the new dialogue about how humans value the natural world of which they are part.

Although the book presents some upbeat material about how biological diversity has been or can be conserved by religious, ethical, or cultural values and beliefs, there are also indications of where there are failures. Moreover, some of these traditional values are eroding in the face of increasing consumerism, and the awe, reverence, taboo, or fear, in most cases, are becoming less effective. The challenge for us today is to reinforce, reinterpret, or reinvent those values that increase human dignity while harmonizing the human-nature interaction.

The chapters that follow are of two kinds – dealing with both the philosophical underpinnings of these human-environment interactions, and with a series of case studies where values derived from religion, ethics, or culture have provided a measure of nature conservation. Chapter 1, written by Professor Denis Goulet, opens up the broad question of "economic development" that is just, real, and sustainable. He uses the term "ethical development," and the integrity and worth of other species is a part of this concept.

Under the title "God and Endangered Species," Professor Holmes Rolston III examines the Christian religious philosophy of nature stewardship and its meaning in Chapter 2.

Dr. Tu Weiming brings the perspective of a scholar of Chinese history and philosophy in Chapter 3. His presentation sheds light on the historical development of the Enlightenment mentality, which has made such an ambiguous impact on both humans and nature, and not just in the modern West. He proposes that a neglect of the idea of "community" has given us a lopsided and somewhat destructive path toward human interactions with humans and human interactions with nature. He holds up the possibility and challenge of developing a more humane, more spiritual and sustainable community drawing upon the cultural and spiritual resources of all religions and indigenous traditions.

Buddhism as a major world religion has had as a central principle a reverence for nature. In Chapter 4, Dr. Leslie Sponsel and Dr. Poranee Natadecha-Sponsel illustrate some of the many ways in which the Buddhist philosophy even today is acting as a major nature conservation force in Thailand in spite of that country's increasing secularization.

Are contemporary Australians moving toward a landscape ecology perception akin to that of the Aborigines of "down under"? Dr. Ranil Senanayake presents some intriguing ideas on this topic in Chapter 5. Perhaps after two centuries of struggle against what was viewed as a hostile environment, there is a recent willingness to learn from the original Australians who had a pervading spiritual dimension to living in a seemingly difficult biophysical environment.

The forested Holy Hills of Xishuangbanna are protected as the abode of the ancestors by the *Dai* people of Yunnan. Dr. Pei Shengji describes in Chapter 6 this situation and its consequences for humans and for biological diversity.

Legends and traditional practices afford a measure of conservation for individual species and for some ecosystems in the island state of Pohnpei in Micronesia, according to Mr. Herson Anson and Mr. William Raynor in Chapter 7. Many of these cultural values promoting nature conservation have persisted in spite of the successive impacts of German, Japanese, and American government, religion, and economics. But traditional values are eroding as Western consumerism and commercialization make increasing inroads.

Chapter 8 by Professor Sonia Juvik presents the results of an interesting research project carried out in the Solomon Islands. She examines the attitudes of those living in different villages, exposed to different forms of Christian theology, toward the natural resources of the Marovo lagoon complex.

In Chapter 9, we obtain insights into traditional native Hawaiian environmental philosophy from Dr. Michael Kioni Dudley. He shows that theirs was a different world view in which the Hawaiian and nature were not really separable entities.

The final chapter by Dr. Ronald Engel sets forth the research and action on the role of ethics, culture, and religion in conserving biodiversity over the past decade. He presents this from his first-hand association with the World Conservation Union, where he headed a task force on ethics and conservation which led to inclusion of this dimension in the *Caring for the Earth* strategy released in October 1991.

REFERENCES

Berry, T. 1992. "The Primordial Imperative." *Earth Ethics* 3(2): 1,3.

FAO. 1990. "FAO Releases New Deforestation Figures." *Tigerpaper* (Bangkok) 17(3): 15 of Forest News.

Hawai'i Audubon Society. 1989. *Hawai'i's Birds*. Honolulu: Hawai'i Audubon Society.

IUCN, UNEP, and WWF. 1991. *Caring for the Earth: A Strategy for Sustainable Living*. Gland, Switzerland: IUCN.

Küng, H. 1991. *Global Responsibility: In Search of a New World Ethic*. New York: Crossroad Publishing.

Raven, P. H. 1988. "Our Diminishing Tropical Forests," in E. O. Wilson, ed., *Biodiversity*. Pp. 119–122. Washington, DC: National Academy Press.

Sohmer, S. H., and R. Gustafson. 1987. *Plants and Flowers of Hawai'i*. Honolulu: University of Hawai'i Press.

Wilson, E. O. 1980. "Species Extinctions ... Resolutions for the 80s." *Harvard Magazine* 82(3): 21.

WRI, IUCN, and UNEP. 1992. *Global Biodiversity Strategy: A Policymakers' Guide*. Washington, DC: World Resources Institute.

WWF. 1986. *The Wild Supermarket: The Importance of Biological Diversity to Food Security*. Gland, Switzerland: World Wide Fund for Nature.

SUGGESTED READING

For further reading on the many aspects of biological diversity:

McNeely, J. A., K. R. Miller, W. V. Reid, R. A. Mittermeier, and T. B. Werner. 1990. *Conserving the World's Biological Diversity.* IUCN, Gland, Switzerland; WRI, CI, WWF-US, and the World Bank, Washington, DC.

Wilson, E. O., ed. 1988. *Biodiversity.* Washington, DC: National Academy Press.

WRI, IUCN, and UNEP. 1992. *Global Biodiversity Strategy: Guidelines for Action to Save, Study, and Use Earth's Biotic Wealth Sustainably and Equitably.* Washington, DC: World Resources Institute.

For data on the status of biodiversity:

World Conservation Monitoring Centre. 1992. *Global Biodiversity.* Cambridge, UK: World Conservation Monitoring Centre.

Chapter 1

BIOLOGICAL DIVERSITY AND ETHICAL DEVELOPMENT

Denis Goulet

INTRODUCTION

In a seminal book on *The Imperative of Responsibility,* the philosopher Hans Jonas (1984) argues that technology has supplanted nature and threatens to destroy nature altogether. Consequently, an ethic of *responsibility for the cosmos* is urgently needed. Jonas claims that such an ethic has never before existed, a debatable point. Whether an ethic of responsibility for the cosmos has ever existed or not, however, it must relativize technology and all development models that equate human progress with technological advance.

One recurring theme in Toynbee's *Study of History* (1965, especially Vol. 1, pp. 59, 379, 382) is the existence of an inverse relationship between the cultural level a society achieves and its technological attainments. Since any human society's psychic energy is limited, when it channels most of it to solve technological problems, little is left for creativity in aesthetic and spiritual domains. The price paid for technological success is often regression on other civilizational fronts.

AN ETHIC OF RESPONSIBILITY: FOUNDATIONS

In the past, major religions constituted human beings as the guardians and stewards of nature. These religions usually trace the origins of nature to a creating God, and in one way or another, they preach to humans a duty of being responsible stewards of nature's goods. In contrast, as the sociologist Peter Berger convincingly shows, modernity has now rendered the world of human knowledge secular, and the religious basis for responsible stewardship has been sapped. Says Berger, "An ethic of responsibility is no longer given, it must be freely chosen." As he explains:

> The English word "heresy" comes from the Greek verb *hairein*, which means "to choose." A *hairesis* originally meant, quite simply, the taking of a choice. A derived meaning is that of an opinion. In the New Testament, as in the Pauline apostles, the word already has a specifically religious connotation that of a faction or party within the wider religious community; the rallying principle of such a faction or party is the particular religious opinion that its members have chosen. Thus in Galatians 5:20 the apostle Paul lists "party spirit" *(hairesis)* along with such evils as strife, selfishness, envy, and drunkenness among the "world of the flesh." In the later development of Christian ecclesiastical institutions, of course, the term acquired much more specific theological and legal meanings. Its etymology remains sharply illuminating.
>
> For this notion of heresy to have any meaning at all, there was presupposed the authority of a religious tradition. Only with regard to such an authority could one take a heretical attitude. The heretic denied this authority, refused to accept the tradition *in toto.* Instead, he picked and chose from the contents of the tradition, and from these pickings and choosings constructed his own defiant opinion. One may suppose that this possibility of heresy has always existed in human communities, as one may suppose that there have always been rebels and innovators. And, surely, those who represented the authority of a tradition must always have been troubled by the possibility. Yet the social context of this phenomenon has changed radically with the coming of modernity: *In premodern situations there is a world of religious certainty, occasionally ruptured by heretical deviations. By contrast, the modern situation is a world of religious uncertainty, occasionally staved off by more or less precarious construction of religious affirmation.* Indeed, one could put this change even more sharply: *For premodern man, heresy is a possibility – usually a rather*

remote one; for modern man, heresy typically becomes a necessity.
Or again, modernity creates a new situation in which picking and
choosing becomes an imperative. (Berger 1980:24–25)

A NEW MODEL OF DECISION-MAKING

Whatever may be the epistemological or theoretical foundation of
such an ethic, its practical expression consists in a decision-making
model that integrates three rationalities. Three distinct rationalities
vie for supremacy in decision-making arenas; they are here personi-
fied as Weberian "ideal" types. According to German sociologist Max
Weber (1968:26), "ideal" types "formulate in conceptually pure form
certain sociologically important types to which social action is more
or less closely approximate." My classification differs from Weber's
own typology since for him rationality was instrumental, value-
centered, affectual, or traditional. For the limited purpose of this
paper, which is to capture the essential dynamics of developmental
decision-making, theoretical classifications forged by Weber and
later theorists – Marcuse, Habermas, and Arendt – are too abstract.
Their typologies were constructed to explain the workings of complex
total societies which embraced competing ideologies or rationalization systems, conflicting subsystems and institutions within society,
and a multiplicity of normative relationships between class interests
and the society at large. To use Marcuse's pithy formula, all theorists
claim that their "rational hierarchy merges with the social one"
(1964:166 cited in Habermas 1970:86).

My aim is not to debate social theory but, more modestly, to
show how conflicting rationalities meet in arenas of development
decision-making. The threefold classification here presented emerges
phenomenologically from observations in these arenas. No effort is
made to devise new abstract categories or to illustrate how Weber's
classical categories apply to the specific field of development.

The rationalities at work in development's decisional arenas
are described in their pure state, although in real life they merge in

various ways. After separate profiles of the three have been drawn, their inter-relationships are illustrated.

Technological Rationality

Technological rationality rests on the epistemological foundations of modern science: it applies scientific knowledge to solving problems or to asserting control over nature, social institutions, technology itself, or people. Its goal is to perform a concrete task like building a dam, clearing a forest, extracting ore from a mine, or boosting the output of a crop. Its animating procedure leads it to treat everything other than the goal instrumentally (i.e., as an aid or obstacle to reaching the targeted goal). Although Weber labels the totality of ends/means thinking as instrumental rationality (*zweckrationalitat*), the qualification "instrumental" is here applied exclusively to the means chosen to reach that goal. Technological instrumental rationalists maintain aids are to be harnessed to the task at hand and obstacles eliminated. Their rationality thus obeys a *hard* logic guided by a calculus of efficiency in the assessment of time or of the utility of any object. It matters little for the technician whether impediments to reaching the goal be material, institutional, or human. Dam engineers who find a hill in their way will dynamite it. If, however, their progress is blocked by bureaucratic red-tape, they will seek to crush or ignore it. If the obstacle is an organized human group, such as a squatters' association that mounts resistance, their technological instincts will dictate not negotiation or compromise, but elimination of the opposition as quickly and efficiently as possible.

Political Rationality

The logic that guides politicians differs both in its goals and in its animating procedures from that of inspiring technicians. Notwithstanding politicians' rhetorical declarations that they are committed to concrete accomplishments, their true goal is to preserve certain institutions and rules of the game or their special power position within those institutions. To illustrate, we may consider a politician elected on the platform promise of constructing 20,000 new low-cost housing units. If, however, while trying to keep the promise, the politician meets with serious opposition criticism from adversaries or financial obstacles the project will be dropped. What truly matters to politicians is *not* building the houses but preserving their own influence and power or that of their party. This explains why political actors so readily compromise, negotiate, accommodate, or engage in what Lyndon Johnson called "horse-trading." I prefer to call it "navigation": politicians navigate between opposite shores, whereas technicians must reach the opposite shore – and this at any price! The procedural spirit of politicians is *soft*, not hard, like that of technological problem-solvers.

Political rationality as described here is exhibited by persons who wield power. Aspirants to power positions are also animated by political rationality; but their logic aims at destroying or altering it, not at maintaining the status quo. Nevertheless, to the extent that such political actors lack power, they do not function as agents of political rationality within arenas of decision-making (see Goulet 1971:334–341). When they challenge the bastions of power, therefore, opposition political actors speak the language of technical or of ethical rationality, even if their ultimate purpose is to gain a platform from which to speak the idiom of political rationality.

Ethical Rationality

The third kind of logic is ethical or humane rationality. This mode of thinking takes as its goal the promotion of values: the creation, nurture, or defence of values considered precious for their own sake – freedom, justice, the inviolability of persons, the "right" of each to a livelihood, dignity, truth, peace, community, friendship, or love. Unlike other forms of rationality just described, the ethical variety takes as its absolute goal – considering all else is relative – the promotion of values, not the performance of concrete tasks or the preservation of institutions or power positions. It is called "ethical" or "humane" rationality because it feeds on moral judgments about what is good and bad, right and wrong, just and unjust.

Ethical rationality draws its themes and its legitimation from two distinct, albeit usually allied, sources. The first is a holistic belief system: a religion, philosophy, world view, symbolic code, or cultural universe of meanings. Its second font is the world of daily life experienced by people lacking power, status, or expertise. These people demand respect as beings of worth independently of their usefulness to others. What in Spanish is called the *vivencia*, or lived experience of ordinary people, convinces them that asserting their dignity as persons is more important than "getting things done," obeying rules, or preserving the status of actors in a power hierarchy or social ladder. For ethical rationality, it is more important *to be* and *to be well* than *to do* or *to be well thought of*. This adherence to values for their own sake determines the procedural spirit of ethical rationality, a spirit which relativizes the goals pursued by other rationalities and treats these instrumentally. Building a road or staying in power is judged by ethical rationality to be good or bad according to whether it helps "unimportant" people gain freedom, respect, or fair treatment.

Although all actors in decisional arenas may be motivated by ethical values in playing their roles, their contributions to rationality mirror their special roles and express the formal warrant they possess for engaging in decision-making. Thus technical experts come to the decision-making table, *not* to promote Utopian visions but to justify their choices on technical grounds. Similarly, "when the chips are down," politicians will bracket their ethical dictates or "place them on hold" and subordinate their technological "good sense" to the requirements of political survival or expediency. If only by default, therefore, the dispossessed or critics of policy become privileged bearers of ethical rationality. In development contexts, those "left out" of power and wealth are the most convincing vectors of ethical rationality because their vital interests can find no basis for expression other than their ethical justification. This category of interlocutors lacks the luxury of grounding its programmatic claims either in efficiency or power maintenance, as other decision-makers do. Figure 1.1 summarizes the goals and procedural spirit of the three rationalities.

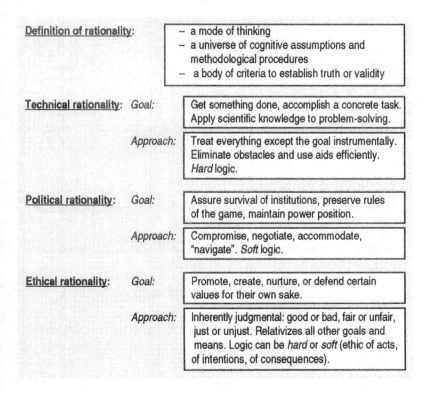

Definition of rationality:		– a mode of thinking – a universe of cognitive assumptions and methodological procedures – a body of criteria to establish truth or validity
Technical rationality:	*Goal:*	Get something done, accomplish a concrete task. Apply scientific knowledge to problem-solving.
	Approach:	Treat everything except the goal instrumentally. Eliminate obstacles and use aids efficiently. *Hard* logic.
Political rationality:	*Goal:*	Assure survival of institutions, preserve rules of the game, maintain power position.
	Approach:	Compromise, negotiate, accommodate, "navigate". *Soft* logic.
Ethical rationality:	*Goal:*	Promote, create, nurture, or defend certain values for their own sake.
	Approach:	Inherently judgmental: good or bad, fair or unfair, just or unjust. Relativizes all other goals and means. Logic can be *hard* or *soft* (ethic of acts, of intentions, of consequences).

Figure 1.1. Definition of rationality and description of three rationalities.

Interaction

When they converge in common decision-making arenas, technological, political, and ethical rationalities impinge upon one another, not in the mode of horizontal mutuality, but at cross-purposes and in a vertical pattern. Each brand of thinking tends to approach the others in triumphal, reductionistic fashion. Technological logic tries to *impose* its vision of goals and animating procedure upon the entire decisional process. Political and ethical rationalities do likewise: each seeks to get the other two "partners" to accept its own favored ground rules of dialogue (see Figure 1.2).

Denis Goulet

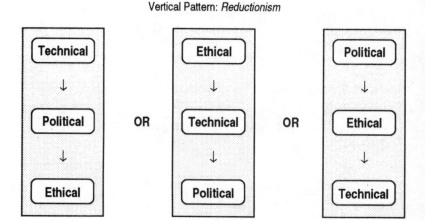

Figure 1.2. Interaction of three rationalities: What is.

Such conflict is guaranteed to produce bad decisions. If technological rationality holds sway, decisions easily prove to be neither
politically feasible nor ethically worthy. Conversely, the triumph of
political logic without due regard for the other rationalities may lead
to decisions which are technically catastrophic or morally repugnant.
Good decisions need to display many qualities, not all of which can
emerge from a unilateral application of a single rationality in decisional
arenas.

The triumphant reductionism just described also prevails in
two other realms of multidimensional discourse far removed from
development decision-making. These are the worlds of religious
ecumenism and of academic interdisciplinarity, where speculative
discourse spills over into practical decisions. In ecumenical religious
debate, at stake are practical ground rules for unification of churches
or, more modestly, terms under which pastoral or liturgical cooperation may occur. In academia, specialists of many disciplines engage
in a quest for integrated pluridisciplinary forms of teaching and

research. Nearly always, however, the fragmented structures of the academy – organized along lines that tend to make absolute the claims of separate disciplines – lead practitioners of each to claim a superior capacity of their own discipline to serve as the unifying axis of pluridisciplinary discourse. The result, in most cases, is either mere juxtaposition of diverse viewpoints or the triumph of one epistemology which asserts itself over the others.

In all three spheres – development decision-making, ecumenical religious discourse, and interdisciplinary academic study – a new model of authentic dialogue is needed where exchanges are circular and reciprocal, not vertical and reductionist. Figure 1.3 illustrates how this circular model might work.

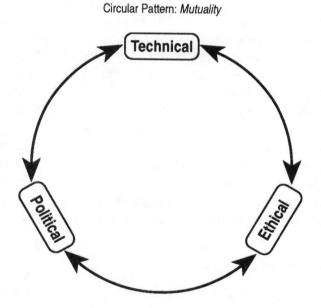

Circular Pattern: *Mutuality*

Assumption: Any form of knowledge is partial and risks mistaking itself for the whole, or dominating discourse with other forms

Figure 1.3. Interaction of three rationalities: What ought to be.

Mutually respectful discourse among diverse rationalities rests on the recognition gained from experience that any kind of knowledge, although partial, risks mistaking itself for the whole (Goulet 1981). Yet, the very partiality of any discipline ought to impose upon its practitioner the obligation to look at the reality under study through alternative sets of cognitive spectacles. One should not assume that one's own intellectual discipline possesses the most "correct" grasp of the common reality studied, but merely that it approaches that reality from one among many possibly valid cognitive vantage points. The entry into these other vantage points, however, must not be conducted in purely extrinsic fashion. Instead one must somehow "get inside" the peculiar spirit of each rationality in the effort to grasp reality as it is known from within the dynamics of many viewpoints. The only proper stance is active respect for other views, allied to modesty regarding the limitations attendant upon one's own preferred vision, and a willingness to reinterpret one's own disciplinary reading of reality in the new light obtained from alternative readings. Such a posture, which is the very antithesis of triumphalism or reductionism, promotes active examination of the epistemological assumptions, procedural preferences, and criteria for norm-setting which place their stamp on all disciplines or special rationalities.

In summary, there exists a logic peculiar to three categories of decision-making actors. In most cases, the demands of their respective rationalities produce either unfruitful conflict or an unwise abdication by one rationality in the face of intellectual aggression by the other. Reductionism and abdication alike generate poor decisions.

UNANSWERED QUESTIONS

I have just argued the need for a new model of decision-making to achieve the new ethic of responsibility for the cosmos. Let me now ᴖose several unanswered questions or unresolved problems which arise around this ethic.

How are we to weight competing ethical values, especially the values of nature's integrity and of preserving plural species with the demands of economic justice? If degrading human poverty is the worst form of pollution, the unanswered question, which can be tested only in the innovative practice of living communities of need, is how to abolish human misery without destroying nature? Do any empirical success stories exist for examination? Jeffrey McNeely of the International Union for Conservation of Nature and Natural Resources has inventoried cases in which nature's integrity has simply been sacrificed, not to economic justice but to the imperative of profit-making. He also identifies successful instances of harmonizing the demands of nature preservation with developmental justice for poor peoples (McNeely 1988).

Second, even if one posits an ethical duty to defend biological diversity, must the survival of any given species be given absolute value or take priority over human needs? One may obviously assign general value to protecting biological diversity without automatically assuming that all flora and fauna must be preserved at any cost. In fact, nature's own evolutionary processes, independently of human activity, have resulted in the disappearance of many biological species over aeons of time. As biologist Daniel Botkin (1991:62) noted, "virtually all wildlife today live in a fragment of what used to be large, often continuous habitats. In today's 'ecological islands,' a species can easily increase rapidly, exhaust its food supply, starve and suffer a rapid decline, meanwhile causing many kinds of harm, sometimes even endangering the survival of other species."

The third unanswered question is the most difficult and the most crucial. Jonas (1984:x), when pleading for a new ethic, writes:

> What we must avoid at all cost is determined by what we must preserve at all cost, and this in turn is predicated on the image of man we entertain. Formerly, this image was enshrined in the teachings of revealed religions. With their eclipse today, secular reason must base the normative concept of man on a cogent, at the least persuasive, doctrine of general being: metaphysics must underpin ethics. Hence, a speculative attempt is made at such an underpinning of man's duties toward himself, his distant posterity, and the plenitude of terrestrial

life under his dominion. That attempt must brave the veto of reigning analytical theory against all attempts of this kind and indeed cannot hope for more than a tentative result. But dare it we must. A philosophy of nature is to bridge the alleged chasm between scientifically ascertainable "is" and morally binding "ought."

The question is whether it is possible to formulate such an ethic in purely rational terms. Is any reason-based ethic powerful enough to override the technological imperative described by Jacques Ellul (1965, 1980, 1990) as the law of what *can* be *must* be?

And can any secularly grounded ethic prove strong enough to override the cash nexus and the "virus of desire" now that all stable dynamisms of desire have been shattered by development's demonstration effects? In trying to formulate such an ethic, Jonas and others seem to confer upon nature absolute rights for its own sake independently of nature's utility to human purposes.

NATURE AND FREEDOM

Robert Vachon (1983:157), a philosopher of intercultural dialogue from Quebec, believes that:

> Orientals, unlike Westerners, do not think of man, nature, and the divine primarily as realities or dimensions which are distinct and autonomous, co-existing face to face with each other. Rather, their vision is non-dualistic, situated between monism and dualism. The Oriental is more concerned with the union, harmony, interconnection, inter-relation and non-duality existing among all dimensions (of being) than with the affirmation of their distinction, inasmuch as for him, life resides rather in the harmony of the whole than in the difference of its parts.

Nature, in short, is the harmony wrought among elements which stand in polar opposition one to the other. For Vachon (1983:160), any holistic vision of reality must grant priority to totality over opposition or polarity.

Viewed in this light, the opposition between human freedom and nature can be subsumed under a larger whole (i.e., integral development, a normative concept embracing three elements: the good life, the optimal foundation of life in society, and the proper stance toward nature and man-made environments). As the French ecologist Bernard Charbonneau (1980a:149–156; 1980b) repeatedly insists, freedom itself is nature, and both form part of a larger whole. And in the words of Daniel Botkin, "Human beings, far from being alien interlopers who disturb the timeless rhythms of nature, are intrinsic elements of the natural order" (Botkin 1991:70).

It is no easy task to reconcile nature and freedom because the emphasis on one or the other has given birth to two divergent ethical orientations. Those who stress the integrity of nature adhere to an ethic whose highest values are the conservation of resources, the preservation of species, and the need to protect nature from human depredations. Those who stress human freedom, in contrast, hold to an ethic whose primary values are justice (which takes the form of an active assault upon human poverty, branded as the worst form of pollution) and the need to "develop" potential resources into their actualized state. Both orientations embrace the same five values: conservation of resources, preservation of species, protection of nature, assault on poverty, and development of resources. What sets the two streams apart is the rank order they assign to these values. A "nature" emphasis locates development and the elimination of human misery below biological conservation and resource protection in the hierarchy of values. Conversely, a "freedom" orientation places development and the active conquest of justice in resource allocation above environmental protection or the preservation of endangered species in the value-scale. In truth, however, all five values should enjoy parity of moral standing. The reason is simply that any long-term, sustainable, equity-enhancing combat against poverty requires wisdom in the exploitation of resources. Yet, the preservation of other species cannot be held out persuasively as a priority goal if the human species is threatened with degrading poverty or extinction. Nature itself is diminished or wounded when its human members are kept "underdeveloped." Reciprocally, these same human members cannot become truly "developed" if their supportive nature is violated.

Perhaps no world view can successfully integrate the requirements of nature and freedom except around some higher *telos*, or end-
value, to which both nature and human freedom are subordinate.
Because neither nature nor freedom can be taken as absolute values,
diverse philosophies and religions assign different value weights to
each. Even within a specific meaning system or world view, competing interpretations arise as to the "proper" weight to be assigned to
each. Indeed, different religions and meaning systems possess diverse
coefficients of insertion in history" (Goulet 1966–67). That is, these
meaning systems are more or less compatible with positive valuations
placed on time, history, and human efforts. To illustrate, Christianity
has throughout its history harbored tendencies both toward exaggerated supernaturalism (in which realms of nature and human activity
are treated merely as arenas in which human beings test their virtue or
save their souls) and, conversely, toward excessive naturalism (in
which God's transcendent and mysterious salvation is reduced simply
to a better way of organizing human society). Similarly, there have
flourished within Christianity schools of interpretation and practices
favoring either an exaggerated God-centered (or theo-centric) kind of
humanism in which it was assumed that anything given to the human
person was stolen away from God or, conversely, favoring an
imbalanced anthropocentric theism in which God became nothing but
a glorified projection of whatever human value enjoyed popularity at
a particular time.

Christianity is often accused of legitimizing ecological irre-
sponsibility. But the exploitative reading of the Genesis command
issued by God to Adam to "Go, multiply and dominate ..." has come
to Christianity only since the Enlightenment. Earlier centuries prac-
tised a reverential respect for nature as the product of God's initial
miraculous creation and of His ever-constant providential care.

To confer upon nature rights for its own sake, independently of
its utility to humans, and to promote a deep ecology philosophy may
create the long-term risk of fostering a new totalitarian fanaticism,
highly reductionist, single-minded, one which somehow provides
ideological justification for running roughshod over human freedom.

DIVERSITY: A REQUIREMENT OF ETHICAL DEVELOPMENT

A case can be made for bio-diversity from the vantage point of development ethics. The bacteriologist René Dubos (1965; cf. Ward and Dubos 1972) argues that the adaptive capacity of the human organism is directly a function of its biological diversity (itself deriving from neurological complexity). Diversity is a general requirement in all living beings for flexible adaptation and survival in adverse conditions. Dubos states that the growing trend toward mass urban settlements poses a severe threat to the capacity of human organisms to survive collectively, if and when their urban support systems are destroyed or damaged. On instrumental grounds he argues that the maintenance of diverse capabilities, which avoid being atrophied by being used in a diversity of environments involving diverse kinds of relationships with nature, is essential to human survival. He further claims that the general lesson taught by evolution is that overspecialized animals quickly die out. His conclusion is that present models of development, of human settlement, of work, and of social organization pose an acute threat to human survival because they are overspecialized and insufficiently diverse.

A second point must be made here, as one constructs the case for bio-diversity from a normative view of development. Is cultural diversity a value for its own sake and, if so, why? Cultures confer upon people their fundamental identity, their meaning, their worth, and their sense of place in the overall cosmic order. Therefore, the active defence of cultural diversity with its varied meaning systems and symbolic beliefs is essential to human development. Cultural diversity is a value for its own sake because free human persons and human communities are values in themselves. Human persons do not live except within cultural communities. Hence if a unitary paradigm of life in community is to be imposed from the requirements of a particular view of technical efficiency, that reductionist model is highly destructive of true development. Leopold Senghor, former president of Senegal, once declared that Africans do not wish to be mere consumers of civilization. Senghor wished to point out that human civilization is not synonymous with contemporary models of modernity predicated on mass urbanism, centralization, industrial consumerism, and environmental destruction.

Moreover, austerity or simplicity in using resources and in bridling aspirations to possess goods is needed in order to shatter technological determinism (see Goulet 1971:255–263; also cf. Fromm 1976 and Elgin 1981). Theravada Buddhists condemn unbridled desire (*Tanha*) because, in their view, it is the cause of misery and unhappiness. Consequently, they seek limits on material development. It may be that the kind of development needed is one open to transcendence, in order to relativize economic growth and technological progress as values, as well as to de-absolutize the claims made by managerial absolutism and the modern nation-state. All those who plead for austerity, simplicity, or limits on consumption and desire favor a respectful attitude toward biological diversity in nature.

They plead, in short, for ethical or authentic development. Two recent formulations of this paradigm of ethical or authentic development are instructive. In September 1986, the Marga Institute held a week-long seminar in Colombo, Sri Lanka, on Ethical Issues in Development. Theorists and practitioners gathered at Marga agreed that any adequate definition of human development must include five dimensions:

1. an economic component dealing with the creation of wealth and improved conditions of material life, equitably distributed;

2. a social ingredient measured as well-being in health, education, housing, and employment;

3. a political dimension including values such as human rights, political freedom, enfranchisement, and some form of democracy;

4. a cultural dimension recognizing that cultures confer identity and self-worth to people; and

5. a full-life paradigm, which refers to meaning systems, symbols, and beliefs concerning the ultimate meaning of life and history (author's notes).

Clearly, environmental soundness must be added to this list.

Some years earlier a seminar on Latin America chose four pairs of words as essential components of development: economic growth, distributional equity, participation/vulnerability, and transcendental values (Pollock 1980). The last two sets of words require explanation. Participation is a decisive voice exercised by people directly affected by policy decisions, whereas vulnerability is the obverse of the participation coin: poor people, regions, and nations must be rendered less vulnerable to decisions that produce external shocks upon them. The words "transcendental values" raise a vital question: "Do people live by GNP alone?" As David Pollock (1980:9) writes:

> Let us assume that a country's economic pie increases. Let us further assume that there is a heightened degree of equity in the way the fruits of that economic pie are distributed. Let us finally assume that decisions affecting production and consumption of the economic pie – nationally and internationally – involve the full participation of all affected parties. Is that the end of the matter? Does man live by GNP alone? Perhaps the latter has been the prevailing line of thought throughout the postwar period since, in the short-run, policy makers must focus primarily upon the pressing issue of increased incomes for the masses; particularly for those below the poverty line. But, despite the obvious importance of such short-run objectives, we should also be asking ourselves other, more uplifting questions. Should we not take advantage of our longer-term vision and ask what kind of person Latin America may wish to evolve by the end of this century. What are the transcendental values – cultural, ethical, artistic, religious, moral – that extend beyond the current workings of the purely economic and social system? How to appeal to youth, who so often seek nourishment in dreams, as well as in bread? What, in short, should be the new face of the Latin American Society in the future, and what human values should lie behind the new countenance?

To Pollock's list, as to Marga's, must also be added environmental soundness.

Contemporary development trends reveal three facets:

1. Economic growth and progress and equitable distribution of the fruits of that growth are occurring only in a small number of countries – the four Asian "tigers" and a few others.

2. For a large number of losers, there is developmental regression, especially in sub-Saharan Africa, Latin America, and Eastern Europe. Countries with heavy foreign debts are particularly hard hit.

3. The third face of contemporary development is the co-existence of micro successes with macro failures. In countries such as Bangladesh and Brazil numerous small-scale, local micro activities may succeed economically, socially, culturally, and institutionally alongside a generalized macro or nationwide failure of development strategies which lead to uncontrolled inflation, massive recession, and increasing dependency on outside economic forces and irreversible destruction of natural riches.

At the very least, the normative views of development just outlined are compatible with the active defence of biological diversity. Not only are they compatible, however; they are the only development paradigms consonant with such defence (see Sachs 1980). The active defence of diversity is an externality which needs to be internalized in carrying out development plans.

Externalities

Economists define an externality as any value or consideration that does not enter a cost-benefit calculus (cf. Okun 1975). Dramatic crises had to erupt before the US public began to understand that factories or weapons dangerously contaminate the atmosphere. Because safety and clean air were treated by corporate policymakers as "externalities" in making production decisions, these values were deemed irrelevant. The social, psychological, and ecological costs of economic or technological activity are never irrelevant, however; they determine the very desirability of that activity. Numerous values formerly treated as externalities need to be internalized if sound social decisions are to be reached.

The principle of responsible internalization is illustrated for auto safety. So long as marketability and luxury appeal were treated as major "internalities," auto designers could treat safety as a mere "externality." They could do likewise with fuel economy if they could plausibly assume that gasoline would remain plentiful and cheap. Once fuel economy became paramount, however, and public pressure grew to provide greater safety in vehicles, new constraints became "internalized," leading to different designs and to a new economic equation for assessing costs and benefits. The broader lesson is clear: *The technological imperative will lead to excessive determinism unless resistance to determinism becomes an internality in any decision about technology* (see Goulet 1989 for detailed justification).

Once the countering of determinism becomes an explicitly internalized goal, planners will conclude that certain technological applications must not be adopted and that others should be slowed down or redirected. Technological development will continue, but it will not be allowed to proceed unchecked on the assumption that it brings only unequivocal benefits. Most decision-makers lack the wisdom to match their sciences, and the beginning of wisdom consists in not rushing headlong into further technological pursuits regardless of social or human costs. At stake, ultimately, is the capacity which any society possesses to absorb technologies that are simultaneously creators and destroyers of social values.

Resisting determinism is not the only externality that needs to be internalized. Other developmental values must also become internalities: equity, cultural diversity, ecological health, and reduced dependency. Societies can begin to harness technology to proper ends only if they understand that technology is simultaneously a universe to be created and an artificial context for their economic and organizational rearrangements. It is difficult to control technology or to dominate nature without damaging it because the Promethean spirit is so powerfully seductive. The domination which this spirit holds out deceives people into treating technological progress as its own justification.

If modern societies continue to treat technology as they have treated nature in the past, they cannot escape technological determinism. Indeed, to adopt a Promethean stance toward technology obliges one to rely on still more technology in order to control technology itself: This is the "technological fix" mentality. We have used technology to conquer nature. Had we respected nature in the past, however, we would have devised technologies quite different from those that we actually produced. We will make similar mistakes in our efforts to moderate technological growth unless we repudiate the stance of untrammelled exploitation. Like nature itself, technology cannot be controlled with impunity unless it is first respected. This is because technology, like nature, dictates its own rhythms. Machines, tools, and computers impose their logic on those who tend them. Analogies abound in the arts. Sculptors respect their tools – chisels and hammers – and musicians their instruments; that the tools and instruments are themselves of human manufacture is no excuse for abusing them. One can learn to respect technologies by designing them to last and to express aesthetic as well as functional values. Such a respectful attitude is the antithesis of the cult of technological obsolescence and of pure functionality which presently dominates. Indeed "developed" societies have ravaged so much of nature's beauty that they cannot live without new forms of technological beauty to take its place. In fact, a minority of architects and designers has always advocated making beauty an "internality" in designing "functional" objects – dwellings, furniture, office equipment, tools, and entire cities. In general, however, such efforts have been viewed by manufacturers and by the public as luxuries. But simplicity, beauty, and durability in everyday technologies are *not* luxuries: They are no less important than utility or efficiency.

A liberating imperative must oppose determinism by making

technological design the choice arena where social-value externalities get internalized.

CONCLUSION

The conclusion flowing from this inquiry into biological diversity and ethical development can be stated as ten theses.

1. Ethical, or authentic, development requires biological diversity.

2. Ethical development also requires cultural diversity.

3. Ethical development requires plural modes of rationality for two reasons:

   • to destroy the monopoly of legitimacy appropriated by scientific and technological rationality, and

   • to integrate technical, political, and ethical rationalities in decision-making in a circular pattern of mutual interaction.

4. Ethical development requires plural models of development. There is no single and necessary path to development predicated on energy-intensive, environmentally wasteful, culturally destructive, and psychologically alienating models of progress.

5. Ethical development requires a nonreductionist approach to economics. As Schumacher (1973) insists in *Small Is Beautiful*, "We must conduct economics as if people mattered."

6. Ethical development requires pluralistic and nonreductionist approaches to technology. Technology is not an absolute value for its own sake which has a mandate to run roughshod over all considerations. As Ellul (1980) urges, we must demythologize technology.

7. Ethical development requires an approach to human beings

which is not exclusively instrumental. Human beings are useful to other human beings and, to some degree, are used as aids in satisfying needs. But human beings have their ultimate worth independently of their instrumental value. Indeed, if one universal value exists in human life, it is that humans are precious for their own sake and on their own terms, independently of their utility to others.

8. The biosphere must be kept diverse both as an instrumental value to render ethical development possible and as a value per se. Like cultural diversity, biological diversity is a value for its own sake, although it is neither a transcendental nor an absolute value. It is, nevertheless, an end value; it has value not merely as a means or as an instrumentality serving human purposes.

9. The question, "Is it possible to have piety toward nature without accountability to nature's creator and to a supreme judge of human affairs?" cannot be answered definitively and absolutely. One recalls, however, that all great religions have preached stewardship of the cosmos and responsibility for nature's integrity and survival based on ultimate human accountability to nature's creator or providential conductor.

10. If ethical development is the only adequate support system for biological diversity, reciprocally, biological diversity is the only support system for ethical development.

REFERENCES

Berger, Peter L. 1980. *The Heretical Imperative.* New York: Anchor Books/ Doubleday.

Botkin, Daniel B. 1991. "Rethinking the Environment, A New Balance of Nature." *The Wilson Quarterly* 15(2): 60–84.

Charbonneau, Bernard. 1980a. *Je Fus, Essai sur la Liberté.* Pau: Imprimerie Marrimpouey Jeune.

Charbonneau, Bernard. 1980b. *Le Feu Vert: Auto-critique du Mouvement Ecologique.* Paris: Editions Karthala.

Dubos, René. 1965. *Man Adapting*. New Haven: Yale University Press.

Elgin, Duane. 1981. *Voluntary Simplicity*. New York: William Morrow.

Ellul, Jacques. 1965. *The Technological Society*. New York: Alfred A. Knopf.

Ellul, Jacques. 1980. *The Technological System*. New York: Continuum.

Ellul, Jacques. 1990. *The Technological Bluff*. Grand Rapids, MI: William B. Eerdmans Publishing.

Fromm, Erich. 1976. *To Have or To Be*. New York: Harper and Row.

Goulet, Denis. 1966–67. "Secular History and Teleology." *World Justice* 8(1): 5–18.

Goulet, Denis. 1971. *The Cruel Choice*. New York: Atheneum.

Goulet, Denis. 1981. "In Defense of Cultural Rights: Technology, Tradition and Conflicting Models of Rationality." *Human Rights Quarterly* 3(4): 1–18.

Goulet, Denis. 1989. *The Uncertain Promise: Value Conflicts in Technology Transfer*. New York: New Horizons Press.

Habermas, Jürgen. 1970. *Toward a Rational Society*. Boston: Beacon Press.

Jonas, Hans. 1984. *The Imperative of Responsibility*. Chicago: University of Chicago Press.

Marcuse, Herbert. 1964. *One Dimensional Man*. Boston: Beacon Press.

McNeely, Jeffrey A. 1988. *Biological Diversity and Human Economy*. Manuscript, second draft, International Union for Conservation of Nature and Natural Resources.

Okun, Arthur M. 1975. *Equality and Efficiency: The Big Tradeoff*. Washington, DC: The Brookings Institution.

Pollock, David H. 1980. "A Latin American Strategy to the Year 2000: Can the Past Serve as a Guide to the Future?" in Vol. 1 (November) of conference proceedings, *Latin American Prospects for the 80's: What Kinds of Development?* Pp. 1–37. Ottawa: Norman Patterson School of International Affairs, Carleton University.

Sachs, Ignacy. 1980. *Strategies de L'Ecodeveloppement*. Paris: Economie et Humanisme et les Editions Ouvrières.

Schumacher, E. F. 1973. *Small Is Beautiful*. New York: Harper and Row.

Toynbee, Arnold J. 1965. *A Study of History*. 10 vols. Abridgement by D. C. Somervell in 2 vols. New York: Dell.

Vachon, Robert. 1983. "Relations de l'homme à la Nature dans les Sagesses Orientales Traditionnelles" in Vol. 9, *Ecologie et Environnement* (Cahiers de Recherche Ethique), Montreal.

Ward, Barbara, and René Dubos. 1972. *Only One Earth*. New York: W. W. Norton.

Weber, Max. 1968. *Economy and Society*. New York: Bedminster Press.

Chapter 2

GOD AND ENDANGERED SPECIES[1]

Holmes Rolston III

RELIGIOUS VALUES AND THE "GOD COMMITTEE"

When the United States Congress lamented the loss of species, they declared that species have "esthetic, ecological, educational, historical, recreational and scientific value to the Nation and its people" (*Endangered Species Act of 1973*). Two further kinds of value that species carry are conspicuously missing in this list; one precedes and one supercedes it, we might say. The first is economic value. Endangered species often have economic value. Economic value is not missing from the paragraph in which these other values of species are named; but rather, in a preceding phrase, economic value is sharply set opposite to them. Congress laments "economic growth and development untempered by adequate concern and conservation" resolves to protect these other, noneconomic values, and has consistently refused to allow the economic benefits or costs of the preservation of a species to be one of the criteria that determines whether it is officially placed on the endangered species list.

The missing value that supercedes the list is religious. Whether Congress would have overstepped its authority to declare that species carry religious value, in addition to the others recounted, is an interesting question. For many persons, this is perhaps the most important value that species carry. A Christian or a Jewish person, while quite endorsing these other values here claimed, will wish to add that these species are also of religious value, and not only to Americans, but to God. Congress could not say that, of course! But defending the freedom of religion, guaranteed in the Constitution, Congress might well have insisted that the species of plants and animals on the continent, which many regard as sacred creation, ought to be conserved because such life is of religious value to the nation and its people.

Though God's name does not appear in the Endangered Species Act itself, it does rather interestingly occur in connection with the Act. The protection Congress has authorized for species is, in principle at least, quite strong. Interpreting the Act, the U. S. Supreme Court insisted "that Congress intended endangered species to be afforded the highest of priorities" (*TVA vs. Hill*). As just noted, "economic" is not among the listed criteria of value; but, since economic costs must sometimes be considered, Congress in 1978 amendments authorized a high-level, interagency committee to evaluate difficult cases, and, should this committee deem fit, to permit human development at the cost of extinction or threatened extinction of species that impede development. This committee is identified by the rather nondescript name, "The Endangered Species Committee"; in the legislation, usually just called "The Committee"; but almost at once it was nicknamed "The God Committee." The name mixes jest with theological insight. It also reveals that religious value is implicitly lurking in the Act, though not explicit in it. God wills for species to continue, subject to natural processes, consonant with human development, and any who will to destroy species in the name of development take, fearfully, the prerogative of God. God's original command here was, "Keep them alive with you" (Genesis 6.19).

It might first seem, at a science congress like this, which is concerned with breeding populations, DDT in food chains, quotas on whales, ivory poaching, debt swaps for nature, and so on, that God is the ultimate irrelevancy. Practical conservation measures are urgent indeed, but there is also a dimension of depth. In fact, when one is conserving life, ultimacy is always nearby. Just because conservation biology is dealing with vital matters, it moves at multiple levels. The practical urgency of on-the-ground conservation is based in a deeper respect for life. Extinction is forever, and when danger is ultimate, absolutes are most relevant. The energies that impel us to save endangered species can and ought to be pragmatic, economic, political, scientific; deep down they are also moral, philosophical, religious.

ADAM, NOAH, AND THE PROLIFIC EARTH

Genesis! Take that word seriously. In the Hebrew creation stories, the "days" (events) of creation are a series of divine imperatives by which Earth is empowered with vitality. "The earth was without form and void, and darkness was upon the face of the deep; and the Spirit of God was moving over the face of the waters. And God said, 'Let there be ...'" (Genesis 1.2–3). "Let the earth put forth vegetation." "Let the earth bring forth living things according to their kinds" (Genesis 1.11, 24). In a memorable phrase, God commands, "Let the waters bring forth swarms of living creatures" (Genesis 1.20). "Swarms" is, I suppose, the earliest Biblical word for bio-diversity!

A prolific Earth generates this teeming life, urged by God, and yet the divine powers move through biological vitality. The Spirit of God is brooding, animating the Earth, and Earth gives birth. Or, as we would now say, Earth speciates. When Jesus looks out over the fields of Galilee, recalling this biological vitality, he comments that "the earth produces of itself" (Mark 4.28); the Greek here says that the Earth produces "automatically," not in a mechanical but in a spontaneous, autonomous, vital sense. That organismic vitality so visibly present has its secret power in the inspiration of God.

God reviews this display of life and finds it "very good." At every step in creation, God blesses this genesis and commands that it continue: "Be fruitful and multiply and fill the waters in the seas, and let birds multiply on the earth" (Genesis 1.22). Or, as we would now say, there is dispersal, conservation by survival over generations, and niche saturation up to carrying capacity. The fauna is included within the covenant: "Behold I establish my covenant with you and your descendants after you, and with every living creature that is with you, the birds, the cattle, and every beast of the earth with you" (Genesis 9.5). In modern terms, the covenant was both ecumenical and ecological. Earth is a promised planet, chosen for abundant life. Adam's first job was a project in taxonomy; he was called to name this swarm of creatures.

The divine imperatives of Genesis are first addressed to the Earth: "Let the earth bring forth vegetation and every living creature." But when humans appear these creation imperatives, executed through Earth's prolific biological powers, also become moral imperatives addressed to humans. They become human duties.

The Bible not only records the first human activity as a project in taxonomy; it also records the first Endangered Species Project – Noah and his ark! The Noah story is quaint and archaic, as much parable as history. Perhaps we should say that, like the creation stories, it records history in parabolic form. Just as the days of creation narrate in prescientific genre a genesis of natural history, the Noah story narrates how God wills for each species on Earth to continue, despite what judgments fall on the wickedness of humans. The fall of humans ought not to bring the fall of creation. Although individual animals perish catastrophically in the flood, God ensures "adequate concern and conservation" at the level of species. The species come through.

After the Flood, the covenant is reestablished with both humans and with the surviving natural kinds: "God said, 'This is the sign of the covenant which I make between me and you and every living creature that is with you, for all future generations: I set my bow in the cloud and it shall be a sign of the covenant between me and the earth'" (Genesis 9.12–13). After the Flood, the command to humans is also repeated: "Be fruitful and multiply, and fill the earth" (Genesis 9.1). But this human development cannot legitimately be at threat to the species, which have just been saved from the Deluge; rather, the bloodlines are protected at threat of divine reckoning (Genesis 9.1–7). The Biblical authors had no concept of genetic species but used instead the vocabulary of bloodlines. The prohibition against eating the blood is a sign of respect for life, and, in this context, protects the forms of life just rescued through the Deluge.

The Endangered Species Act and the God Committee are contemporary events. Beside that we have to set in comparison, contrasting markedly in its archaic form, but superceding the Act in the depths of its insights, this Ark of God conserving species for their religious value. Noah is not told to save those species that are of "esthetic, ecological, educational, historical, recreational and scientific value" to people. He is commanded to save them *all*, when they are threatened by human corruption. After the Flood, plants were again given for food, and permission to eat animals as well.

Today, preservation of species is routinely defended in terms of human benefits. From a utilitarian viewpoint, species have medical, agricultural, and industrial possibilities. They can be used for scientific study; they can be enjoyed recreationally. Even species that are not directly useful may be indirectly useful for the roles they occupy in ecosystems, adding resilience and stability. High quality human life requires a high diversity of species.

All these humanistic justifications for the preservation of species, although correct and required as part of endangered species policy, fall short of Noah's environmental ethics. These are good reasons but not the best, because they do not value these species for what they are in themselves, for what they are in God. They are inadequate for either Hebrew or Christian faith, neither of which is simply humanistic about species. Noah was not simply conserving global stock. A human is not the measure of things. What is taught in the Noah story is sensitivity to forms of life and the biological and theological forces producing them. What is required is not human prudence but principled responsibility to the biospheric Earth. Indeed, for monotheists, this is principled responsibility to God.

Many of these Genesis stories are archaic in two senses. First, they are old and couched in now outmoded thought forms; second, they are about archaic or aboriginal truths: creation, imaging God, the primeval sin, being a brother's keeper, building the tower of Babel and storming the gates of heaven, Abraham's call, Israel's struggle with God. The Noah story is archaic in both these senses, the genre is antiquated, but the Noah threat is imminent and at the foundations. One form of life has never endangered so many others. The story is a kind of anomaly in the Scriptures, because we do not believe that humans in ancient times endangered large numbers of species. The story is a kind of myth teaching a perennial reverence for life, and the ancient myth today, for the first time ever, has become tragic fact. Never before has this level of question been faced. Humans have more understanding than ever of the speciating processes, more predictive power to foresee the intended and unintended results of their actions, and more power to reverse the undesirable consequences. If there is a word of God here, lingering out of the primordial past, it is "Keep them alive with you" (Genesis 6.19).

Such a command is given to biologists, to politicians, to citizens, and the command is to theologians as well. Facing the next century, indeed turning the millennium, not only have biologists become convinced that conservation is vital, there is growing conviction among theologians that theology has been too anthropocentric. The nonhuman world is a vital part of Earth's story. It is now increasingly obvious that environmental welfare is an inescapable part of our global agenda.

Biology and theology are not always easy disciplines to join, and we shall have more to say about that. But one conviction they do share in common is that the ecosystemic Earth is prolific. Seen from the side of biology, this is called speciation, biodiversity, selective pressures for adapted fit, maximizing offspring in the next generation, niche diversification, species packing, carrying capacity, and the like. It may even be called selfish (self-actualizing) genes or ruthless survival of the fittest. Geneticists and population biologists model a maximizing of offspring in the next generation; they track sets of genes or a species over time. Evolutionary ecologists see new arrivals as well as survivals; they observe niche ramification and increase of kinds.

Seen from the side of theology, this trend toward diversity is a good thing – a godly thing. This fertility is sacred. Nature is a projective system; Earth broods swarms of creatures that are very good. In a more modern idiom, Earth is value-able, able for value, a system that generates valuable life. This genesis is, in biological perspective, "of itself," spontaneous, autonomous; and biologists find nature to be prolific, even before the God question is raised. Afterward, theologians wish to add that when you discover that you live in such a startling, prolific world, explanations may not be over until one detects God in, with, and under it all.

RESOURCES AND SOURCES

In Genesis, the stories of human sources quickly mix with stories about human resources: "Behold, I have given you every plant yielding seed which is upon the face of all the earth, and every tree with seed in its fruit; you shall have them for food" (Genesis 1.29). The couple are commanded to dress the garden and till it; there are ample rivers; there is gold and onyx stone (Genesis 2.10). "And the Lord God made for Adam and his wife garments of skins, and clothed them" (Genesis 3.21). At least after the Flood, animals are given as food, as well as plants. So there is no contesting that genesis requires resources. There is ecology here that supports an economy.

But the story is about our sources as much as our resources. In terms of the two kinds of values that we tried earlier to locate with reference to the Endangered Species Act, the economic values are recognized but entwined with religious values. If some of these species are good for food (or for medicine, or industry), certainly Genesis warrants saving them on such account, but Genesis teaches this peripherally to a more central teaching that the values carried by species are vitally sacred. Christians have often and admirably focussed on economic values where humans have been unjustly deprived of these (jobs, food, shelter, health care). But in endangered species legislation, Christians should insist that these values should take their place if and only if creation remains in place. The values that Christians wish to defend are often the softer, more diffuse ones, and also the deeper, foundational ones essential to an abundant life. Perhaps God wills a good life in a promised land; but without its fauna and flora, the land cannot fulfill all its promise.

One cannot look to the market to produce or protect the multiple values that the nation and its people enjoy from the myriad species inhabiting the continent, since many of these values carried by species are not, or not simply, economic ones. A pristine natural system, with its full complement of species, is a religious resource, as well as a scientific, recreational, aesthetic, or economic one. So we can call these species resources if we like. But there is more. If they are nothing but our human resources, it seems to profane them, to forget the pleasure that their Creator takes in this creation. Species are more than resources, instrumental to civilization, more than even a religious resource. The species on the landscape are instance and evidence of the primeval, wild, creative source of Earth and all its natural kinds. That is why, in confrontation with wildness, humans know the sense of the sublime. We get transported by forces awful and overpowering, by the signature of time and eternity.

Being among the archetypes, a landscape, a forest, a sea swarming with its kinds is about as near to ultimacy as we can come in the natural world – a vast scene of birth and death, sprouting, budding, flowering, fruiting, passing away, passing life on. We feel life's transient beauty sustained over chaos. In a wildlife sanctuary, especially a sanctuary for endangered species, Christians recognize God's creation, and others may find the Ultimate Reality or a Nature sacred in itself.

Nature, swarming with its kinds, is a wonderland, a miracle. "Praise the Lord from the earth you sea monsters and all deeps, fire and hail, snow and frost, stormy wind fulfilling his command! Mountains and all hills, fruit trees and all cedars! Beasts and all cattle, creeping things and flying birds!" (Psalm 148.8–9) "Thou crownest the year with thy bounty; the tracks of thy chariot drip with fatness. The pastures of the wilderness drip, the hills gird themselves with joy, the meadows clothe themselves with flocks, the valleys deck themselves with grain, they shout and sing for joy" (Psalm 65.11–13).

In contrast with the surrounding religions from which Biblical faith emerged, the natural world is disenchanted; it is neither God, nor is it full of gods; but it remains sacred, a sacrament of God. Though nature is an incomplete revelation of God's presence, it remains a mysterious sign of divine power. The birds of the air neither sow nor reap, yet are fed by the heavenly Father, who notices the sparrows that fall. Not even Solomon is arrayed with the glory of the lilies, though the grass of the field, today alive, perishes tomorrow (Matthew 6). There is in every seed and root a promise. Sowers sow, the seed grows secretly, and sowers return to reap their harvests. God sends rain on the just and unjust. "A generation goes, and a generation comes, but the earth remains forever" (Ecclesiastes 1.4).

RANDOMNESS AND CREATIVITY

We said earlier that it is not always easy to join biology and theology. To put that problem in a contrasting pair of keywords: Is Earth by "design" or "accident"? Before Darwin, the world seemed well designed, species were adapted for their niches, fixed in kind, going back to an original special creation. Just as watches indicated a watchmaker, rabbits indicated a rabbitmaker, creatures indicated a Creator. But Darwin found random mutations, blind to the needs of the organism, a surplus of offspring, the inevitable survival of the acci-dentally better adapted, the evolution of species, and no original creation at all. Rather, evolutionary history is the cumulation of a billion years of accident and groping. On the retention side, natural selection preserves the adapted fits, to be sure; but on the supply side, the innovations are random. The secret of life, once lodged in the Spirit of God, lies in fact in biochemistry, in DNA, where these forms of life, stumbled upon over the millennia, are microscopically coded for coping in the macroscopic world.

Rather than God's first creating and subsequently preserving all of Earth's teeming species, species have come and gone in a constant and sometimes catastrophic turnover. The five million or so species now inhabiting Earth are less than 1 percent of five billion or so species that across ages past have entered and exited natural history, sometimes by random walk, sometimes by drift, always by struggle to survive, never by divine design. A species is a discrete biological form of life that has arisen opportunistically. All species, *Homo sapiens* included, are here by luck. Earth is not a watch but a jungle; not a well-designed Eden, rather a contingent chaos.

Chaos is the buzzword in a number of sciences these days, but we must handle this concept with care. In addition to randomness in genetic mutations, there is indeterminacy in physics, turbulence in hydraulics, the Beijing effect in climatology (by which a butterfly fluttering in Beijing can trigger a storm in California), data scatter in statistics, and even mathematical chaos. Jacques Monod, a Nobel prizewinner, has claimed in a best-selling book that natural history is "an enormous lottery presided over by natural selection, blindly picking the rare winners from among numbers drawn at utter random" (Monod 1972). Recently, David Raup (1988) has put catastrophism back into paleontology, and Stephen Gould (1989) has learned from the Burgess shale that the species on Earth, however wonderful, are chance riches and accidental life. If so, there can be no connection between God and species of whatever kind, much less endangered species.

Although there is indeterminacy in physics, perhaps we should notice that cosmology is finding that this universe is spectacularly fine-tuned for life. If biology and theology are sometimes difficult to join, physics and theology are quite congenial now. The anthropic principle (somewhat unfortunately named, really a biocentric principle) finds dozens and even hundreds of microphysical and astronomical phenomena, both contingencies and necessities, that have to be almost exactly what they are if life is to be possible. Examples are the charges on electrons and protons, the strengths of the four binding forces, the scales, distributions, and ages of the stars, the expansion rate of the universe, the proportions of hydrogen and helium, the structures of the heavier elements, and so on. Even before there is life, we already get a pro-life universe out of physics.

If the contingencies and necessities of physics make life possible, so also do its indeterminacies. For just these microphysical indeterminacies provide the openness in physical nature upon which a biological organism can superimpose its program. The organism is fine-tuned at the molecular level to nurse its way through the quantum states by electron transport, proton pumping, selective ion permeability, and so on. The organism interacts with the microphenomena (somewhat analogously to the way physicists participate in their observations), catching the random fluctuations to its advantage, setting up from above the conditions of probability. The organism via its information and biochemistry participates in forming the course of the microevents that constitute its passage through the world. Physics frees the world for the adventure of biology.

That adventure is the historical evolutionary epic. The difference between physics and biology is that biology is a historical science, an earthbound science, where there are cumulative historical discoveries coded into the organism over time. The laws of physics and chemistry are the same on Jupiter, on Mars, in the galaxy Andromeda. But genetic coding, the cytochrome C molecule, the citric acid cycle, photosynthesis, trilobites, dinosaurs, and grizzly bears are peculiar to Earth. They incorporate elements of randomness, but even more they represent creative achievement on planet Earth, biological vitality now coded into the DNA and expressed in these forms of life we call species. Perhaps we are beginning to see that "accident" is not the full story; rather there is a particular and precious creativity at work on our planet.

Jacques Monod may think that life is an enormous accident, but George Wald, also a Nobel prizewinner, thinks differently: "This universe breeds life inevitably" (1974:9). Manfred Eigen, still another Nobel laureate, concludes "that the evolution of life ... must be

considered an *inevitable* process, despite its indeterminate course"
(1971:519). Life is destined to come as part of the narrative story, yet
the exact routes it will take are open and subject to historical vicissi-
tudes. Melvin Calvin, still another Nobel laureate, concludes that life
evolves "not by accident but because of the peculiar chemistries of the
various bases and amino acids. ... There is a kind of selectivity
intrinsic in the structures (1975:176)." So far from being random, life
is "a logical consequence" of natural principles.

It is admittedly difficult to get clear about this. Despite the pro-
life world given to us in physics and chemistry, there is not much in
the atoms themselves that enable us to predict that they will organize
themselves in this remarkable way. Given physics and chemistry as a
premise, there is no deductive or inductive logic by which biology
follows as a conclusion. Still there is this remarkable story to tell, and,
when it happens, though it is no inference, neither does it seem just an
accident. There does seem to be some creativity intrinsic in the Earth,
a prolific tendency by which these elements order themselves up to
life.

The system does prove to be pro-life; the story goes from zero
to five million species in five billion years, passing through perhaps
five billion species which have come and gone en route. There is a
mixture of inevitability and openness, so that one way or another,
given the conditions and constants of physics and chemistry, together
with the biased earthen environment, life will somehow both surely
and surprisingly appear. Once upon a time there was a primitive
planetary environment in which the formation of living things had a
high probability; or, in other words, the archaic Earth was a pregnant
Earth. On this Mother Earth we may not so much need interference by
a supernatural agency as the recognition of a marvelous endowment
of matter-energy with a propensity toward life. Yet this endowment
can be congenially seen, at a deeper level, as the divine creativity.

Order is mixed with disorder, and the living forms of order
require subroutines of disorder. A crystal has lots of order, simple,
spatial order, sameness, but no life. Biological systems have lots of

order too, but of a richer kind, functional complexity, organization, diverse parts coordinated in a whole, mobile, autonomous, self-informed process. This kind of high order needs a certain looseness (disorder, randomness, indeterminacy) if there is to be novelty, mutation, evolution, creative growth, if there is to be defence of life before a mixedly certain and uncertain environment, a cyclic but also historically developing environment. There can now be exploratory cybernetic systems, the adventure of life. There can be speciation.

Chance is not necessarily an ultimate explanation, not usually an explanation that ends all other explanations. It is often a confession of ignorance, and there may be signals in the "noise" that seem random, signals that our model is as yet incompetent to detect. Once upon a time, in fact, signals did appear in the noise. Where once there was matter, energy, and where these remain, there appeared information, symbolically encoded, and life. There emerged a new state of matter, neither liquid, nor gaseous, nor solid, but vital. Randomness does not rule out creativity, randomness plus something to catch the upstrokes, something to code them and pass them on to the future, such randomness yields creativity, at the same time that it puts adventure, freedom, drama, and surprise into the storied evolutionary course.

The word "design" nowhere occurs in Genesis, though the concept of creativity pervades the opening chapters. There is divine fiat, divine doing, but the mode is an empowering permission that places productive autonomy in the creation. "Let Earth bring forth ..." Biologists cannot deny this creativity; indeed, better than anyone else biologists know that Earth has brought forth the natural kinds, prolifically, exuberantly over the millennia. When we examine this creativity, the better question is not so much whether these creatures have *design* in the craftsman/architect – artifact/machine sense as whether they have *value*. Do they have a kind of inherent goodness? A thing does not have to be directly intended to have value. It can be the systemic outcome of a searching, problem-solving process. If so, it results from creativity; it is a valuable achievement.

STRUGGLE AND PERPETUAL PERISHING

Perhaps the contrasting keywords that make joining biology and religion problematic are not so much "design" and "accident" as they are "good" versus "evil." Darwin once exclaimed that the evolutionary process was "clumsy, wasteful, blundering, low, and horribly cruel" (Darwin, in de Beer 1962). That is antithesis indeed to the Genesis verdict of "very good." The Darwinian revolution has discovered that the governing principle is survival in a world thrown forward in chaotic contest: "nature red in tooth and claw" (Tennyson 1850, Part LVI, Stanza 4). Nature is a wilderness that contains only the thousandth part of creatures that sought to be, but rather became seeds eaten, young fallen to prey or disease. The wilderness swarms with kinds, as Genesis recognizes, but is a vast graveyard with a hundred species laid waste for one or two that survive. Blind and ever urgent exploitation is nature's driving theme, the survival of the fittest.

Here there is no compassion, no love, no caring, no concern. The process is not designed by a benevolent god; to the contrary it is ungodly. In a famous exclamation, remembered now for a century, T. H. Huxley (1893:83) reacted that the values society most cherishes depend "not on imitating the cosmic process, still less in running away from it, but in combating it." George Williams, a foremost student of natural selection, has recently intensified the same conclusion: "Thus, brought before the tribunal of ethics, the cosmos stands condemned. The conscience of man must revolt against the gross immorality of nature" (Williams 1988).

Biologists are not altogether comfortable with the word "struggle," often preferring the notions of "adaptedness" and "fitness." There is as much interdependence as there is contest. Still, plenty of "struggle" remains in biology, and can it be godly? We do have to begin with the fact that life is the first miracle that comes out of Earthen nature, and death is a secondary one. For an organism, for a species, things can go wrong just because they can go right; a rock or a river never fails, but then again neither can ever succeed. In biology, we are not just dealing with causes and effects but with vitality and survival. A rock exists on its own, having no need of its environment, but an organism has interests and welfare; it must seek resources. Biological creativity is logically entwined with struggle and perpetual perishing. Life decomposes and recomposes. Generation means re-generation.

The Buddhists, though they find no God, discover the first noble truth that life is suffering; and they reverence life none the less for its struggle. Perhaps we ought to conserve endangered species, but not because speciation is godly. But then again, perhaps we are making a category mistake. Nature is, we have already concluded, evidently prolific, and religion, monotheism included, seldom if ever teaches that creativity is without struggle. Life, according to the Psalmist, is green pastures found in the valley of the shadows, a table prepared in the midst of enemies. Genesis by the third chapter is teaching that we eat our bread in sweat and tears. Life pushes on in the midst of its perpetual perishing.

In physics and chemistry there is, as we said, no history folding and refolding itself into compounding chapters in the story; that comes with the evolutionary epic of biology on Earth. In physics and chemistry there is also no suffering; that comes also in biology. The shadow side of life is death. Even in presentient life there is struggle and duress, and, with the evolution of sentience, there is suffering. The energies of physics deepen through time into the pain of biology. Conservation in physics and chemistry is a foregone conclusion (e.g., conservation of energy, mass, baryon number, or spin). Conservation in biology is vital and contingent. Life can be lost, indeed it invariably is – at least individual life is, although by reproducing and speciating life is conserved over the millennia.

Indeed, the death of earlier creatures makes room for later ones, room to live and, in time, to evolve. If nothing much had ever died, nothing much could have ever lived. The evolutionary adventure is propagated onward, using and sacrificing particular individuals, which are employed in, but readily abandoned to, the larger currents of life. The pro-life evolution both overleaps death and seems impossible without it. The element of struggle is muted and transmuted in the systemic whole. Something is always dying, something is always living on.

There is always some providential power by which life persists over the vortex of chaos. We find life handed on, through ills and all, by wisdom genetically programmed, as well as in the cultural heritage of our forebears. The secret of life is only penultimately in the DNA, the secret of life is this struggling on, this struggling through to something higher. We dimly comprehend that we stand the beneficiaries of a vast providence of struggle that has resulted in the panorama of life. It is just that sense of ongoing life, transcending individuality, that makes life at the species level a religious value. The sacred character of life is its struggling beauty. Speciation lies at the core of life's brilliance, and to confront an endangered species, struggling to survive, is to face a moment of eternal truth. Life is always an endangered species, and it survives by the power of God.

NATURE, LAW, AND GRACE

Paradoxically, past the suffering, life is a kind of gift. Every animal, every plant has to seek resources, but life persists because it is provided for in the system. Earth is a kind of providing ground. Life is a suffering through to something higher, which, seen from an earthy side, seems to be random chance, but seen from a godward side, is divine creativity. Each species is a bit of brilliance, a bit of endurance, a moment of truth, animated, spirited inventiveness. The swarms of creatures are not so much an ungodly jungle as a garden Earth, a divinely inspired Earth. Design is not the right word; it is a word borrowed from mechanics and their machines, watchmakers and their clocks. An organism is not a machine, not a clock. Genesis is the word we want; it is a word with "genes" in it, with the gift of autonomy and self-creation. Designed machines do not have any interesting history; clocks have no story lines. But organisms must live story lines, and that epic is life lived on in the midst of its perpetual perishing, life arriving and struggling through to something higher. That story continues for several billion years; such an Earthen providing ground is, in the theological perspective, providential.

Providential adventures do not so much have design as do they have pathways. In grace accompanying a passage through history, there must be a genetic pathway available, during the traveling of which survival can be maintained, and along which phenotypes can be produced in a sequence that gets from here to there by increments, some of which may be quantum increments, which natural selection can see. There has to be a lineage of descent, ascent, exploration, adventure. There has to be a story line over which the new skills or structures can be achieved. It is not enough that there be ideal form; there must be history that can reach the form. Monotheists who take Genesis seriously, who take creation vitally, do not suppose a *Deux ex machina* that lifts organisms out of their environment, redesigns them, and reinserts them with an upgraded design. Rather they find a divine creativity that leads and lures along available routes of Earth history.

Laws are important in natural systems, but natural law is not the complete explanatory category for nature, any more than is randomness and chance. In nature, beyond the law is grace. There is creativity by which more comes out of less. Actually, science does not handle historical explanations very competently, especially where there are emergent novelties; science prefers lawlike explanations in which there are no surprises. One predicts, and the prediction comes true. But nevertheless biology is full of unpredictable surprises. The account of natural history will not be by way of implication, whether deductive or inductive. There is no covering law (such as natural selection), plus initial conditions (such as trilobites), from which one can deduce primates, any more than one can assume microbes as a premise and deduce trilobites in conclusion. Nor is there any induction (expecting the future to be like the past) by which one can expect trilobites later from procaryotes earlier, or dinosaurs still later by extrapolating along a regression line (a progression line!) drawn from procaryotes to trilobites. There are no humans invisibly present (as an acorn secretly contains an oak) in the primitive eucaryotes, to unfold in a lawlike or programmatic way. All we can do is tell the epic story – eucaryotes, trilobites, dinosaurs, primates, persons who are scientists, ethicists, conservation biologists – and the drama may prove enough to justify it.

The epic story is of swarms of these wild creatures, as well as of the humans who come late in the story and have a remarkable oversight of the swarming landscapes and seas. Although Adam and Noah are, in a sense, trustees of the creation, Job finds it amply evident that the nonhuman creation is wild, outside the hand of humans, outside culture. In God, animals are born free. "Who has let the wild ass go free? Who has loosed the bonds of the swift ass, to whom I have given the steppe for his home, and the salt land for his dwelling place? He scorns the tumult of the city; he hears not the shouts of the driver. He ranges the mountain as his pasture, and he searches after every green thing" (Job 39.5–8). Even in Bible times, the wild ass was something of an endangered species; it persisted in Palestine nevertheless until 1928, when it became extinct.

"Is it by your wisdom that the hawk soars, and spreads his wings toward the south? Is it at your command that the eagle mounts up and makes his nest on high? On the rock he dwells and makes his home in the fastness of the rocky crag. Thence he spies out the prey; his eyes behold it afar. His young ones suck up blood; and where the slain are, there is he. ... Shall a faultfinder contend with the Almighty? He who argues with God, let him answer it" (Job 39.26–40.2). "The high mountains are for the wild goats; the rocks are a refuge for the badgers. ... The young lions roar for their prey, seeking their food from God. ... O Lord, how manifold are thy works! In wisdom hast thou made them all; the earth is full of thy creatures" (Psalm 104.18–24).

Though outside the hand of humans, the wild animals are not outside both divine and biological order. The Creator's love for the creation is sublime precisely because it does not conform to human purposes. Wild animals and wild flowers are loved by God for their own sake. That God is personal as revealed in interhuman cultural relations does not mean that the natural relationship of God to hawks and badgers is personal, nor should humans treat such creatures as persons. They are to be treated with appropriate respect for their wildness. The meaning of the words "good" and "divine" is not the same in nature and in culture.

Just as Job was pointed out of his human troubles toward the wild Palestinian landscape, it is a useful, saving corrective to a simplistic Jesus-loves-me;-this-I-know, God-is-on-my-side theology, to discover vast ranges of creation that now have nothing to do with satisfying our personal desires, and that there were eons of evolutionary time that had nothing to do even with satisfying human desires. What the wildlands with their swarms of species do "for us," if we must phrase it that way, is teach that God is not "for us" humans alone. God is "for" these wild creatures too. God loves wildness as much as God loves culture, and in this love God both blesses and satisfies wildness and also leaves it to its own spontaneous autonomy. To be self-actualizing under God is a good thing for humans, and it is a good thing, mutatis mutandis, for coyotes and columbines. That is the blessing of divinity in them. That the world is nothing but human resource, with nature otherwise value free, is sometimes taken to be the ultimately modern conviction, following which we will become fully human and be saved. It is in fact the ultimate in fiction, where the sin of pride comes around again to destroy.

In Earth's wildness there is a complex mixture of authority and autonomy, a divine imperative that there be communities (ecosystems) of spontaneous and autonomous ("wild") creatures, each creature defending its form of life. A principal insight that Biblical faith can contribute, beyond constraints on the exploitation of wildlife, is a forceful support of the concept of wildlife refuges or "sanctuaries" in national policy. A wildlife sanctuary is a place where nonhuman life is sacrosanct, that is, valued in ways that surpass not only economic levels but even in ways that transcend resource use in the ordinary senses. In that sense Christian conviction wants sanctuaries not only for humans, but also for wildlife. This is true for all wildlife; there is hardly a stretch of landscape in our nation that is not impoverished of its native fauna and flora. It is even more true for endangered species.

CREATIVITY AND CREATOR

Religious persons can bring a perspective of depth on biological conservation. They will see species as a characteristic expression of the creative process. Confronting endangered species, as when in a wilderness or at sea, the realities of nature cannot be ignored. The swarms of species are both presence and symbol of forces in natural systems that transcend human powers and human utility. Like earth, air, fire, and water, the fauna and flora, Earth's original natural systems are a kind of archetype of the foundations of the world. The central "goods" of the biosphere – forests and sky, sunshine and rain, rivers and earth, the everlasting hills, the cycling seasons, wildflowers and wildlife, hydrologic cycles, photosynthesis, soil fertility, food chains, genetic codes, speciation and reproduction, succession and its resetting, life and death and life renewed – were in place long before humans arrived.

We want a genetic account in the deeper sense, one that tells the full story of the historical genesis of value. The history of Earth, we are claiming, is a story of the achievement, conservation, and sharing of values. Earth is a fertile planet, and in that sense, fertility is the deepest category of all, one classically reached by the category of creation. In fact, what is there is a systemic process, profoundly but partially described by evolutionary theory, a historical saga during which spectacular values are achieved and at the core of which the critical category is value (not selfishness), commonly termed "survival value," better interpreted as valuable information, coded genetically, that is apt for "living on and on" (*sur-vival*), for coping, for life's persisting in the midst of its perpetual perishing. Such fecundity is better interpreted still as divine creativity.

Although this history has been a struggling through to achieve something higher (which evolutionary theory can only model as better adapted fit), there is no particular cause to assume that the grim accounts of it are the adult, biologically correct ones, and the gracious, creative, charismatic ones are childish, naive, or romantic. Indeed the latter accounts are romantic in the classical sense, the adventurous epic of life lived and loved in its rich historical novelty.

From a biological point of view, several billion years worth of creative toil, several million species of teeming life have been handed over to the care of this late-coming species in which mind has flowered and morals have emerged. From a political point of view, the American nation inherits a continent over which life has flowed for a thousand times as long as the nation itself has yet lasted. From a theological point of view, humans threaten the divine creation. These species belong not to us, either as persons or as a nation, but to God. There is something un-Christian, something ungodly, about living in a society where one species takes itself as absolute and values everything else relative to its national or personal utility. It is more than appropriate for Christians to call for humans to respect the plenitude of being that surrounds us in the wild world, once so vast and now so quickly vanishing.

There can no longer be found about 500 faunal species and subspecies that have become extinct in the United States since 1600, and only rarely found another 500 species that are (officially or unofficially) threatened and endangered. In the American West, 164 fishes are endangered, or vulnerable and of concern. About 56 percent of fish species in the United States and Canada are in need of protection. About 70 percent of the endangered and threatened fishes of the world are in North America. About 14 percent of the native continental United States flora, approximately 3,000 taxa, are either endangered or approaching endangerment. About 100 native plant taxa may already be extinct. In Hawai'i, of the 2,200 native taxa, about 40 percent is in jeopardy and 225 species are believed extinct. Even where not nationally in danger, once-frequent species are locally extinct or rare. Utah, California, Texas, Oregon, Arizona, Nevada, Florida, and Michigan stand to lose plant species numbered in the hundreds. On global scales, about 20 percent of plant and animal species are projected to be lost within a few decades.

What on Earth are we doing? Humans cannot know what they

are doing on Earth unless they also know what they are undoing. They can and ought to create their cultures, under God; but this ought not to be by undoing creation.

RELIGIOUS CONSERVATION BIOLOGISTS

Whatever you may make of God, biological creativity is indisputable. There is creation, whether or not there is Creator, just as there is law, whether or not there is a lawgiver. Sometimes biologists decline to speak of creation, because they fear a Creator lurking in the concept of creation. Well, at least there is genesis, whether or not there is a Genitor. Ultimately, there is a kind of creativity in nature demanding either that we spell nature with a capital *N*, or pass beyond nature to nature's God. Biologists today are not inclined, nor should they be as biologists, to look for explanations in supernature, but biologists nevertheless find a nature that is super! Superb! Science teaches us to eliminate from nature any suggestions of teleology, but it is not so easy for science to talk us out of genesis. What has managed to happen on Earth is startling by any criteria. Biologists may doubt whether there is a Creator, but no biologist can doubt genesis.

In this deeper sense, says Ernst Mayr, though hostile enough to traditional monotheism, "virtually all biologists are religious, in the deeper sense of the word, even though it may be a religion without revelation. ... The unknown and maybe unknowable instills in us a sense of humility and awe" (1982:81). "And if one is a truly thinking biologist, one has a feeling of responsibility for nature, as reflected by much of the conservation movement" (Mayr 1985:60). "I would say," concludes Loren Eiseley, at the end of *The Immense Journey*, "that if 'dead' matter has reared up this curious landscape of fiddling crickets, song sparrows, and wondering men, it must be plain even to the most devoted materialist that the matter of which he speaks contains amazing, if not dreadful powers, and may not impossibly be ... 'but one mask of many worn by the Great Face behind'" (1957:210). In a stunning volume of photographs and existential reflections produced by the space explorers, a pivotal and repeated theme is the awe experienced at the first sight of the whole Earth (Kelley 1988). Though these hundred and more astronauts come from many cultures and countries, their virtually unanimous experience is religious, of being grasped, shaken, and transformed by an astonishing encounter. Viewing the fertile Earth, they get in space something of the experience that biologists get in time – a glimpse of divinity.

Annie Dillard, who herself can be religious enough in other moments, is sometimes terrified at the evolutionary ordeal. Overlooking the long and odious scene of suffering and violence, she cries out: "I came from the world, I crawled out of a sea of amino acids, and now I must whirl around and shake my fist at that sea and cry shame" (Dillard 1974:177). Must she? There is nothing shameful about amino acids rising out of the sea, speciating, swarming over Earth, assembling into myriads of species, not the least of which is *Homo sapiens*, with mind to think and hand to act. If I were Aphrodite, rising from the sea, I think I would turn back to reflect on that event and raise both hands and cheer, rather than shake a fist in shame. And if I came to realize that my rising out of the misty seas involved a long struggle of life renewed in the midst of its perpetual perishing, I might well fall to my knees in praise. Nature is not some kind of night and darkness; exactly the opposite: "Nature is one vast miracle transcending the reality of night and nothingness" (Eiseley 1960:171).

When J. B. S. Haldane found himself in conversation with some theologians and was asked what he had concluded from his long studies in biology about the character of God, he replied that God had an inordinate fondness for beetles. God must have loved beetles; he made so many of them. But species counts are only one indication of diversity, and perhaps the fuller response is that God must have loved life; God animated such a prolific Earth. Haldane went on to say that the marks of biological nature were its "beauty," "tragedy," and "inexhaustible queerness" (Haldane 1932:167–169). This beauty approaches the sublime; the tragedy is perpetually redeemed with the renewal of life, and the inexhaustible queerness recomposes as the numinous. Biology produces many doubts; here are two more. I doubt whether you can be a conservation biologist without a respect for life, and the line between respect for life and reverence for life is one that I doubt that you can always recognize. If anything at all on Earth is sacred, it must be this enthralling creativity that characterizes our home planet. If anywhere, here is the brooding Spirit of God.

Just this vitality is now so vulnerable; the life that has been spontaneously, divinely conserved over the millennia is now at stake, urgently. This too is the experience of the astronauts, shared with conservation biologists. For whatever biologists may make of the mystery of life's origins, they too virtually unanimously conclude that the catastrophic loss of species that is at hand, that is by our hand, is tragic, irreversible, and unforgivable. Difficult to join though biology and theology sometimes are, they are difficult to separate in their respect for life. Earlier we worried that the processes of creation might be ungodly. But faced with extinction of these processes, biology and theology quickly couple to reach one sure conclusion. For humans to shut down Earth's prolific creativity is ungodly.

NOTE

1. This article will also be published in *Biodiversity and Landscapes* edited by K. C. Kim and R. D. Weaver, Cambridge University Press, New York, 1994. Reprinted by permission of the publisher.

REFERENCES

Calvin, Melvin. 1975. "Chemical Evolution." *American Scientist* 63:169–177.

de Beer, Gavin. 1962. *Reflections of a Darwinian.* London: Thomas Nelson and Sons.

Dillard, Annie. 1974. *Pilgrim at Tinker Creek.* New York: Harper's Magazine Press.

Eigen, Manfred. 1971. "Self-organization of Matter and the Evolution of Biological Macromolecules." *Die Naturwissenschaften* 58:465–523.

Eiseley, Loren. 1957. *The Immense Journey.* New York: Vintage Books, Random House.

Eiseley, Loren. 1960. *The Firmament of Time.* New York: Atheneum.

Gould, Stephen Jay. 1989. *Wonderful Life: The Burgess Shale and the Nature of History.* New York: W. W. Norton.

Haldane, J. B. S. 1932 [1966]. *The Causes of Evolution.* Ithaca: Cornell University Press.

Huxley, Thomas H. 1893 [1947]. "Evolution and Ethics," in T. H. Huxley and Julian Huxley, *Evolution and Ethics.* London: Pilot Press.

Kelley, Kevin W., ed. 1988. *The Home Planet.* Reading, MA: Addison-Wesley.

Mayr, Ernst. 1982. *The Growth of Biological Thought.* Cambridge: Harvard University Press.

Mayr, Ernst. 1985. "How Biology Differs from the Physical Sciences," in David J. Depew and Bruce H. Weber, eds., *Evolution at a Crossroads: The New Biology and the New Philosophy of Science.* Pp. 43–63. Cambridge: MIT Press.

Monod, Jacques. 1972. *Chance and Necessity.* New York: Random House.

Raup, David M. 1988. "Changing Views of Natural Catastrophe," in *The Great Ideas Today 1988.* Pp. 55–77. Chicago: Encyclopedia Britannica.

Tennyson, Alfred Lord. 1850. *In Memoriam A. H. H.*

Wald, George. 1974. "Fitness in the Universe: Choices and Necessities," in J. Oró, S. L. Miller, C. Ponnamperuma, and R. S. Young, eds., *Cosmochemical Evolution and the Origins of Life.* Pp. 7–27. Dordrecht, Netherlands: D. Reidel Publishing.

Williams, George. 1988. "Huxley's Evolution and Ethics in Sociobiological Perspective." *Zygon* 23:383–407.

Chapter 3

TOWARD THE POSSIBILITY OF A GLOBAL COMMUNITY

Tu Weiming

In response to the "Challenges in Contemporary Spirituality," I, as a student of Asian and comparative religion, made the following observation:

> We need an ethic significantly different from the social Darwinian model of self-interest and competitiveness. We must go beyond the mentality that the promise of growth is limitless and the supply of energy is inexhaustible. The destructiveness of "secular humanism" lies not in its secularity but in its anthropocentrism. While the recognition of the spirituality of matter helps us to appreciate human religiosity as a way of living the fullness of life in all its dimensions, the exclusive focus on humanity as the measure of all things or as endowed with the unquestioned authority of dominion over nature relegates the spiritual realm to irrelevance and reduces nature to an object of consumption. The human project has been so impoverished that the answer to "What is man that thou art mindful of him?" is either want or greed. The crisis of modernity is not secularization per se but the inability to experience matter as the embodiment of spirit (*Local Knowledge, Ancient Wisdom,* edited by Steven Friesen, East-West Center, 1991, pp. 2–3).

My observation was occasioned by a powerful image: the celestial vision of the earth, the stunningly beautiful blue planet as seen through the eyes of the astronauts. The image presents two significantly different realities. The unprecedented scientific and technological achievement that enables us not only to survey literally all boundaries of the good earth but even to measure the thickness of the air we breathe is certainly an established fact. Yet, a more compelling actuality is the realization: how precious and precarious this lifeboat of ours is in the midst of the turbulent ocean of galaxies. This realization, heightened by a poetic sensitivity and infused by a religious sense of awe, impels us to recognize as professionals as well as concerned citizens of the world that we ourselves now belong to the category of endangered species. This poignant recognition is deduced from the obvious fact that we have mercilessly polluted our own habitat.

We may gaze at the distant stars, but we are rooted here on earth and have become acutely aware of its vulnerability and increasingly wary of its fragility. The imagined possibility of creating a new habitat for the human community on an unknown planet by massive emigration has lost much of its persuasive power even in science fiction. The practical difficulty of developing alternative sources of energy and the virtual impossibility of inventing radically different forms of life make us realize how unique is our life on earth. As the horizon of our knowledge extends, we learn that there are limits to the speed and quantity of our economic growth, that natural resources are exhaustible, that the deterioration of our environment has disastrous consequences for the human community as a whole, that the serious loss of genes, species, and ecosystems is endangering the equilibrium of our life-support system, and that a minimum condition for continuous human survival requires the actual practice of sustainable life in highly industrialized societies. The painful acknowledgment that what we have been doing to nature in the last two centuries since the French Revolution, especially in the last four decades since the Second World War, which has resulted in a course of self-destruction has instilled in us a sense of urgency. Indeed, by poisoning the air we breathe and the water we drink, in short, by degrading our environment, we are recklessly reducing the livability of our habitat to a point of no return. The necessity of a basic reorientation of our thought with a view toward a fundamental restructuring of our life-style is glaringly clear.

Tools and methods specifically designed to reduce the magnitude of environmental degradation, such as recycling aluminum and applying pollution control technology, are now readily available. The concern for halting the trend toward massive destruction of biodiversity has prompted new frontiers of research in ecological science. Furthermore, in economics, the emerging field of ecological-economics has already recommended ways for using economic manipulations in favor of conservation. However, as Larry Hamilton poignantly reminds us, "They do not get at the cause of the problem." Far-sighted ecologists, engineers, economists, and earth scientists, intent on developing a communal critical self-consciousness for "saving spaceship earth," have made an appeal to poets, priests, artists, and philosophers for their active participation in this intellectual and spiritual joint venture to make our habitat, our home, safe for generations to come. The symposium, which led to this book, focused on ethics, values, and religions as ways of "caring for the planet and reducing its rate of impoverishment"; it diagnostically and prognostically addressed issues pertaining to conserving biological diversity. In this paper, I would like to address the destructive power of these "transnational, transgenerational, and transideological" assaults on the environment. Taking the Enlightenment mentality as a point of departure, I hope to bring some understanding to a major paradox as we reflect upon our human condition in a way scientifically disinterested and yet profoundly personal.

The Enlightenment mentality underlies the rise of the modern West as the most dynamic and transformative ideology in human history. Virtually all major spheres of interest characteristic of the modern age are indebted to or intertwined with this mentality: science and technology, industrial capitalism, market economy, democratic polity, mass communication, research universities, civil and military bureaucracies, and professional organizations. Furthermore, the values we cherish as definitions of modern consciousness including liberty, equality, human rights, dignity of the individual, respect for privacy, government for, by, and of the people, and due process of law are genetically, if not structurally, inseparable from the Enlightenment mentality. We have flourished in the spheres of interest and their attendant values occasioned by the advent of the modern West since the Enlightenment of the eighteenth century. They have made our lifeworld operative and meaningful.

We are so seasoned in the Enlightenment mentality that we assume that the reasonableness of its general ideological thrust is self-evident. The Enlightenment faith in progress, reason, and individualism may have lost some of its persuasive power in the modern West, but it remains a standard of inspiration for intellectual and spiritual leaders throughout the world. It is inconceivable that any modern project, including those in ecological sciences, does not subscribe to the theses that the human condition is improvable, that it is desirable to find rational means to solve the world's problems, and that the dignity of the person as an individual ought to be respected. Enlightenment as human awakening, as the discovery of the human potential for global transformation, and as the realization of the human desire to become the measure and master of all things is still the most influential moral discourse in the political culture of the modern age; for decades it has been the unquestioned assumption of the ruling minorities and cultural élites of the developing countries, as well as the highly industrialized nations.

A fair understanding of the Enlightenment mentality requires a frank discussion of the dark side of the modern West as well. The "unbound Prometheus," symbolizing the run-away technology of development, may have been a spectacular achievement of human ingenuity in the early phases of industrial revolution. Despite impassioned reactions from the Romantic movement and insightful criticisms by the forefathers of the "human sciences," the Enlightenment mentality fueled by the Faustian drive to explore, to know, to conquer, and to subdue persisted as the reigning ideology of the modern West.

By the late nineteenth century, the Enlightenment mentality revealed itself as "knowledge is power" (Francis Bacon), "the historical inevitability of human progress" (August Comte), or "the humanization of nature" (Karl Marx), and it had become an intellectual source for social Darwinian competitiveness. This competitive spirit, justified by a simple-minded reading of the principle of "the survival of the fittest" in turn provided a strong rationale for imperialism. To be sure, according to Max Weber, the rise of the modern West owes much to the Protestant ethic which historically engendered the spirit of capitalism in Western Europe and North America. Nevertheless, modernization, as rationalization, is Enlightenment mentality to the core. Faith in progress, reason, and individualism propelled the modern West to engulf the world in a restless march toward modernity. As the Western nations assumed the role of innovators, executors, and judges of the international rules of the game defined in terms of competition for wealth and power, the stage was set for growth, development, and exploitation. The unleashed juggernaut blatantly exhibited unbridled aggressiveness toward humanity, nature, and itself. This unprecedented destructive engine has for the first time in history made the viability of the human species problematical.

The realization that the human species may not be viable and that human life as lived in the last two centuries has explosive potential for destroying the entire life-support system has prompted some reflective and concerned minds in the natural sciences, social sciences, and humanities to join forces in a concerted effort to think through the issue in the broadest term possible, and to act immediately and concretely in order to bring about realizable incremental results.

The spirit of "thinking globally and acting locally" enables us to put the *Problematik* at hand in proper perspective. Values espoused by the French Revolution, namely liberty, equality, and fraternity, as well as the aforementioned progress, reason, and individualism embedded in the Enlightenment mentality, are an integral part of our heritage. We do well to recognize the persuasiveness of these values throughout the world and to affirm our commitment to them for giving meaning to our cherished form of life. The lamentable situation that these values are being realized only in Western Europe and North America must not be used as an excuse to relegate them to a culturally specific and thus parochial status. Notwithstanding the tremendous difficulty of spreading these values to other parts of the world, the potential of their universalizability is widely acknowledged. The most formidable defenders of these values are not necessarily in Paris, London, or New York; they are more likely to be in Beijing, Moscow, or Johannesburg.

A brief look at what Talcott Parsons defined as the three inseparable dimensions of modernity two decades ago will help to sharpen our focus on the issue. Despite the acknowledgment that it has taken centuries for democracy to flourish in England, France, or the United States and that the forms it has taken in these societies are still seriously flawed, democracy as a standard of inspiration has universal appeal. Moreover, the "third wave of democracy" is a major transformative force in international politics. A more powerful dynamic can be seen working in the competitive markets. The disintegration of communist Eastern Europe and the collapse of the Union of Soviet Socialist Republics clearly indicate the strength of democratic polity and market economy in defining the process of modernization. Although individualism, Parsons' third dimension of modernity, is less persuasive, it seems to symbolize an ethos underlying the entire value system of the modern West.

While we are willing to grant that the modernization project as exemplified by the modern West is now the common heritage of humanity, we should not be blind to the serious contradictions inherent in the project and the explosive destructiveness embodied in the dynamics of the modern West. The legacy of the Enlightenment is pregnant with disorienting ambiguities. The values it espouses do "not cohere as an integrated value system recommending a coordinated ethical course of action." The conflict between liberty and equality is often unresolvable. It may not be farfetched to suggest, in grossly simplified terms, that while capitalist countries embraced principles of liberty to organize their political life, communist societies articulated the rhetoric of equality to impose their ideological control. The matter is greatly complicated by the deliberate attempts of the capitalist countries to employ socialist measures, ostensibly to blunt the hard edges of free enterprise but, in reality, to save capitalism from collapsing since the end of the First World War.

Classical liberalism, as brilliantly developed by Friedrich von

Hayek, has performed an invaluable service to elucidate the dangers of socialism as a "road to serfdom," but its own role and function in providing both theoretical and practical guidance to advanced capitalism are quite limited. The idea of competitive market or free enterprise, in Adam Smith's sense, may have been a motive force and ideological weapon in the modernizing process, but it has never been fully implemented as a political or economic institution. In fact, the exponential growth of the central government, not to mention the ubiquity of the military bureaucracy, in all Western democracies has so fundamentally redefined the insights of the Enlightenment that self-interest, expansion, domination, manipulation, and control have supplanted seemingly innocuous values such as progress, reason, and individualism. A realistic appraisal of the Enlightenment mentality reveals many faces of the modern West incongruous with the image of "the Age of Reason." In the context of modern Western hegemonic discourse, progress means inequality, reason means self-interest, and individualism means greed. The American dream of owning a car and a house, earning a fair wage, and enjoying freedom of privacy, expression, religion, and travel, while reasonable to our sense of what ordinary life entails, is lamentably unexportable as a modern demand from a global perspective.

An urgent task for the community of like-minded persons deeply concerned about ecological issues is to ensure that both the ruling minorities and cultural élites in the modern West actively participate in this spiritual joint venture to rethink the Enlightenment heritage. The paradox is, we cannot afford to uncritically accept its inner logic in light of the unintended negative consequences it has engendered for the life-support system; nor can we reject its relevance, with all of the fruitful ambiguities it entails, to our intellectual self-definition, present and future. There is no easy way out. We do not have an "either-or" choice. The possibility of a radically different ethic or a new value system separate from and independent of the Enlightenment mentality is neither realistic nor authentic. It may even appear to be either cynical or hypercritical. We need to explore the spiritual resources that may help us to broaden the scope of the

Enlightenment project, deepen its moral sensitivity, and, if necessary, creatively transform its genetic constraints in order to fully realize its potential as a world view for the human community as a whole.

A key to the success of this spiritual joint venture is to recognize the conspicuous absence of the idea of community, let alone the global community, in the Enlightenment project. Fraternity, a functional equivalent of community in the three cardinal virtues of the French Revolution, has received scanty attention in modern Western economic, political, and social thought. The willingness to tolerate inequality, the faith in the salvific power of self-interest, and the unbridled affirmation of aggressive egoism have greatly poisoned the good will of progress, reason, and individualism. The first step in creating a new world order is to articulate a universal intent for the formation of a global community. This requires, at a minimum, the replacement of the principle of self-interest, no matter how broadly defined, with a new golden rule: "Do not do unto others what you would not want others to do unto you." Since the new golden rule is stated in the negative, it will have to be augmented by a positive principle: "In order to establish myself, I must help others to establish themselves; in order to enlarge myself, I have to help them to enlarge themselves." An inclusive sense of community, based on the communal critical self-consciousness of the reflective and concerned ecological minds, may emerge as a result.

The mobilization of three kinds of spiritual resources is necessary to ensure that this simple vision be grounded in the historicity of the cultural complexes informing our ways of life today. The first kind involves the ethico-religious traditions of the modern West, notably Greek philosophy, Judaism, and Christianity. The very fact that they have been instrumental in giving birth to the Enlightenment mentality makes a compelling case that they re-examine their relationships to the rise of the modern West in order to create a new public sphere for the transvaluation of typical Western values. The exclusive dichotomy of matter/spirit, body/mind, sacred/profane, man/nature, or creator/creature must be transcended to allow supreme values such as the sanctity of the earth, the continuity of being, the beneficiary interaction between the human community and nature, and the mutuality between humankind and heaven to receive the saliency they deserve in philosophy and theology.

The Greek philosophical emphasis on rationality, the Biblical image of man having "dominion over the fish of the sea, and over the fowl of the air, and over every living thing that moveth upon the earth," and the so-called Protestant work ethic provided necessary, if not sufficient, sources for the Enlightenment mentality. However, the unintended negative consequences of the rise of the modern West have so undermined the sense of community implicit in the Hellenistic idea of the citizen, Judaic idea of the covenant, and the Christian idea of universal love that it is morally imperative for these great traditions, which have maintained highly complex and tension-ridden relationships with the Enlightenment mentality, to formulate their critique of the blatant anthropocentrism inherent in the Enlightenment project.

The second kind of spiritual resource is derived from non-Western axial-age civilizations which include Hinduism, Jainism, and Buddhism in South and Southeast Asia, Confucianism and Taoism in East Asia, and Islam. These ethico-religious traditions provide sophisticated and practicable resources in world views, rituals, institutions, styles of education, and patterns of human-relatedness. They can help to develop forms of life, both as continuation of and alternative to the Western European and North American exemplification of the Enlightenment mentality. Industrial East Asia, under the influence of Confucian culture, has already developed a less adversarial, less individualistic, and less self-interested modern civilization. The co-existence of market economy with government leadership, democratic polity with meritocracy, and individual initiatives with group orientation has made this region economically and politically the most dynamic area of the world since the Second World War. The implications of the contribution of Confucian ethics to the rise of industrial East Asia for the possible emergence of Hindu, Jain, Buddhist, and Islamic forms of modernity are far-reaching. The Westernization of Confucian Asia (including Japan, the two Koreas, mainland China, Hong Kong, Taiwan, Singapore, and Vietnam) may

have forever altered its spiritual landscape, but its indigenous resources (including Mahayana Buddhism, Taoism, Shintoism, sha-
manism, and other folk religions) have the resiliency to resurface and
make their presence known in a new synthesis. The caveat, of course,
is that, having been humiliated and frustrated by the imperialist and
colonial domination of the modern West for more than a century, the
rise of industrial East Asia symbolizes the instrumental rationality of
the Enlightenment heritage with a vengeance. Indeed, the mentality of
Japan and the Four Mini-Dragons is characterized by mercantilism,
commercialism, and international competitiveness. Surely, the possibility of their developing a more humane and sustainable community
should not be exaggerated, nor should it be undermined.

The third kind of spiritual resource involves the primal traditions: native American, Hawaiian, Maori, and numerous tribal indigenous religious traditions. They have demonstrated, with physical
strength and aesthetic elegance, that human life has been sustainable
since the Neolithic age. The implications for practical living are far-
reaching. Their style of human flourishing is not a figment of the mind
but an experienced reality in our modern age.

I am proposing that, as both beneficiaries and victims of the
Enlightenment mentality, we show our fidelity to our common heritage by enriching it, transforming it, and restructuring it with all three
kinds of spiritual resources still available to us for the sake of
developing a truly ecumenical sense of global community. The papers
in this book, while divergent in their methodological approaches and
different in their ethical and religious orientations, are all serious
attempts to identify and tap the spiritual resources available in the
human community for inspirational guides to find a way out of our
predicament: the road to liberation may mislead us to the dark cave of
an "endangered species." It may not be immodest to say that we are
beginning to develop a fourth kind of spiritual resource from the core
of the Enlightenment project itself. Our disciplined reflection, a
communal act rather than an isolated struggle, is a first step toward the
"creative zone" envisioned by religious leaders and ethical teachers.

Chapter 4

THE POTENTIAL CONTRIBUTION OF BUDDHISM IN DEVELOPING AN ENVIRONMENTAL ETHIC FOR THE CONSERVATION OF BIODIVERSITY

Leslie E. Sponsel and Poranee Natadecha-Sponsel

INTRODUCTION

In recent years two usually divergent paradigms – the humanities and the sciences – have converged on the same point: that although science, technology, economy, and government are necessary components for the conservation of biodiversity, they are insufficient. Also needed are values, and some of these may be found in religion (e.g., Bodhi 1987:vi; Sandell 1987b:2). In a discussion of environmental ethics, philosopher Shrader-Frechette (1981:28) asserts: "How to view man's relationship to the environment is one of the great moral problems of our time." Shrader-Frechette (1981:ix) also observes:

> If environmental degradation were purely, or even primarily, a problem demanding scientific or technological solutions, then its resolution would probably have been accomplished by now. As it is, however, our crises of pollution and resource depletion reflect profound difficulties with some of the most basic principles in our accepted system of values. They challenge us to assess the adequacy of those principles and, if need be, to discover a new framework for describing what it means to behave ethically or to be a "moral" person.

Several contributors to the volume titled *Biodiversity* edited by Wilson (1988) call for the development of values for the conservation of biodiversity. For example, biologist Paul Ehrlich (1988:22) states: "A quasi-religious transformation leading to the appreciation of diversity for its own sake, apart from the obvious direct benefits to humanity, may be required to save other organisms and ourselves." On September 29, 1986, in the Basilica of Saint Francis of Assisi in Italy, as part of its 25th Anniversary Celebration, the World Wildlife Fund International organized a conference of religious leaders to identify from the doctrine of their respective faiths some basic principles for the development of environmental ethics. This was published as *The Assisi Declarations: Messages on Man and Nature from Buddhism, Christianity, Hinduism, Islam, and Judaism* (WWFI 1986). Another example of a benchmark is the publication edited by McNeely et al. (1990:26), *Conserving the World's Biological Diversity*, wherein eight principles were identified as an ethical basis for conserving biodiversity. These principles have been quoted verbatim, but they have been reordered and given a heading by the present authors. (These will be discussed in the next section.)

AN ETHICAL BASIS FOR CONSERVING BIODIVERSITY

1. *Unity*:

   Humanity is part of nature, and humans are subject to the same immutable ecological laws as all other species on the planet. All life depends on the uninterrupted functioning of natural systems that ensure the supply of energy and nutrients, so ecological responsibility among all people is necessary for the survival, security, equity, and dignity of the world's communities. Human culture must be built upon a profound respect for nature, a sense of being at one with nature and a recognition that human affairs must proceed in harmony and balance with nature.

2. *Interdependence*:

The world is an interdependent whole made up of natural and human communities. The well-being and health of any one part depends upon the well-being and health of the other parts.

3. *Limits*:

The ecological limits within which we must work are not limits to human endeavor; instead, they give direction and guidance as to how human affairs can sustain environmental stability and diversity.

4. *Sustainability*:

Sustainability is the basic principle of all social and economic development. Personal and social values should be chosen to accentuate the richness of flora, fauna, and human experience. This moral foundation will enable the many utilitarian values of nature – for food, health, science, technology, industry, and recreation – to be equitably distributed and sustained for future generations.

5. *Diversity*:

Diversity in ethical and cultural outlooks toward nature and human life is to be encouraged by promoting relationships that respect and enhance the diversity of life, irrespective of the political, economic, or religious ideology dominant in a society.

6. *Rights*:

All species have an inherent right to exist. The ecological processes that support the integrity of the biosphere and its diverse species, landscapes, and habitats are to be maintained. Similarly, the full range of human culture adaptations to local environments is to be enabled to prosper.

7. *Responsibility*:

The well-being of future generations is a social responsibility of the present generation. Therefore, the present generation should limit its consumption of nonrenewable resources to the level that is necessary to meet the basic needs of society, and ensure that renewable resources are nurtured for their sustainable productivity.

8. *Individual*:
All persons must be empowered to exercise responsibility for their own lives and for the life of the earth. They must therefore have full access to educational opportunities, political enfranchisement, and sustaining livelihoods (McNeely et al. 1990:26; reprinted by permission of the publisher).

Although the *Assisi Declarations*, among other sources, indicate the potential of many religions to contribute to the development of an environmental ethic for conserving biodiversity, the great religions of Asian civilizations seem to be of special relevance (Callicott and Ames 1989b; Goldsmith 1988; see Table 4.1).[1] Moreover, Galtung (1988:108–111) argued that Buddhism is closer to nature than the other major religions because more parts of nature are considered sacred. Philosopher Skolimowski (1990:29) mentions that only after he published his book *Eco-Philosophy: Designing New Tactics for Living* (1981) did he realize that embedded within it was the Buddhist Eightfold Path. Buddhism is ecocentric rather than anthropocentric or theocentric. Since at least the 1970s many articles and books have been published on the relevance of Buddhism to ecology and conservation.[2]

Sponsel and Natadecha (1988) argued that Buddhism may help solve the problem of deforestation and thus reduce the loss of biodiversity, for at least four reasons: (1) environmental ethics are inherent in Buddhism; (2) many of the principles of Buddhism and ecology are in accord; (3) there is a long history of mutualism between Buddhism and trees and forests; (4) in recent years a revitalization of Buddhism has started in Thailand, which has been linked with conservation and other environmental concerns including the problem of deforestation.

EASTERN	WESTERN
Hinduism	**Judaism**
Buddhism	**Christianity**
Taoism	**Islam**
Confucianism	
Shinto	
Oriented toward nature	Oriented toward history
Conceives of Divine Power(s) as impersonal	Conceives of Divine Power(s) as personal
Places little emphasis on time	Places great emphasis on time
Believes world and man eternal and uncreated	Believes world and man created and not eternal
Believes truth is not bound to particular persons	Believes truth comes through particular persons
Tends to be inclusive	Tends to be exclusive
Has little interest in clearly defined doctrine	Has strong interest in clearly defined doctrine
Tends toward unity of reality	Tends toward duality of reality
Downgrades individual will	Exalts individual will

Table 4.1. Comparative religion
Source: Monk et al. 1987:49. Reprinted by permission of
Prentice-Hall, Englewood Cliffs, New Jersey.

We will develop the first point further as a focus for the present paper on the potential contribution of Buddhism to developing an environmental ethic for conserving biodiversity. Then we will briefly update the situation in Thailand with an emphasis on recent conservation efforts by Buddhist monks and villagers. The rest of this paper is divided into three parts: ideas, actions and consequences, and conclusions.

Our basic thesis is that environmental ethics are inherent in Buddhism and readily identifiable, but that modernization has undermined adherence to Buddhism in nations like Thailand, and precipitated an unprecedented environmental crisis, including the reduction of forests and associated biodiversity. The real problem is how to encourage a closer fit of actions to ideals so that the consequences will be less destructive and more adaptive. This problem has been addressed with some success in certain regions of Thailand in recent years by monks who remain, as traditionally, among the most important leaders in local communities, and who have become environmental activists.

IDEAS

Buddhism is a philosophy with religious associations which has endured for more than 2,500 years (Lester 1987). Although the Buddhists of the world represent only about 6 percent of humanity, they number about 311,438,000. More than 99.5 percent of Buddhists are in Asia where they are concentrated in the Southeast and East. However, Buddhism is found in 86 countries of the world (*Britannica Book of the Year 1990*) with at least 18 variations.

Disregarding the variation in Buddhist ideas and practices, at the generic level there are interesting similarities and differences between the environmental ethics, which are inherent in Buddhism, and the eight points proposed by McNeely et al. (1990) as a basis for the development of an ethic for conserving biodiversity. (For the core principles of Buddhism, see Table 4.2.)[3]

.

Table 4.2. (opposite) Core principles of Buddhism
Modified from Galtung 1988.

The Four Noble Truths

1. Life is discontinuity, dissatisfaction, suffering
2. The cause is ignorance and craving (including greed)
3. The cure is reduction of ignorance and craving
4. The prescriptions are in the Noble Eightfold Path

The Noble Eightfold Path

1. Right understanding of the Four Noble Truths
2. Right thought – aims, will, values, motives, goals
3. Right speech – polite, kind, and considerate
4. Right action – being an example for others
5. Right livelihood – making a living the right way
6. Right effort – diligence
7. Right mindfulness – enduring attentiveness
8. Right concentration – meditation

The Five Negative Precepts

1. Abstain from taking life – nonviolence
2. Abstain from taking what is not given
3. Abstain from adultery and sexual misconduct
4. Abstain from lying
5. Abstain from intoxicating substances

The Five Positive Precepts

1. Compassion
2. Good vocation – no making or selling of weapons or intoxicants
3. Control of sexual life and pleasures
4. Telling the truth
5. Attentiveness, mindfulness, care

The Triple Refuge

1. The Buddha – but avoid idolatry
2. The Dhamma – the teachings of the Buddha
3. The Sangha – the community of monks

The Three Marks

1. Impermanence – everything is always arising and ceasing
2. Suffering – discontinuity, imbalance, dissatisfaction
3. Non-self – no enduring, separate self

The Four Needs

1. Food
2. Clothing
3. Shelter
4. Medicine

Unity and Interdependence

In Buddhism humans are an integral part of the natural system (Sandell 1987a:32). Buddhism focuses on the interaction of mind and nature through three key practices: direct knowledge, discriminating awareness, and deep compassion (Kaza 1990:22). Kaza (1990) explains:

> By cultivating these three practices, one's actions in relation to the environment come to be based in relationship and interconnectedness, rather than in dualistic subject-object modes of separation. Through this approach, one's orientation to the world is fundamentally altered from dominant species to member of a community, from part to process (p. 22).

> With interdependence as a core understanding, an environmental ethic becomes a practice in recognizing and supporting relationships with all beings. The Buddhist practitioner is then responsible for speaking out against acts of environmental abuse with a voice that is born out of deep and intimate knowing (p. 24).

As Capra (1980:132) remarked, "We can never speak about nature without, at the same time, speaking about ourselves." The Buddhist must transcend separateness and identify with the welfare of all beings in nature (Smith 1958:118). Indeed, *nirvana*, the awakening into a state of bliss, is reached when the boundary separating the finite self from its surroundings and also all mortal cravings are extinguished (Smith 1958:125, 131). Buddhism is monistic rather than dualistic in its assertion of the fundamental unity of self and environment rather than in dichotomizing organism and environment or human and nature (Barash 1973:215; Komin 1985:173; Thurman 1984:100, 103). As Kaza (1990:25) aptly states: "An environmental ethic is not something we apply outside ourselves; there is no outside ourselves. We are the environment, and it is us."

The laws of nature apply to humans as well as to other living beings (Komin 1985:175). Indeed, the Buddha's teaching, the *Dhamma*, refers to the discovery of the nature of things, which encompasses the character and processes of the natural environment (Rajavaramuni

1985:57). "The luminous contemplation of the realities of nature is the very heart of the Buddhist experience," according to Thurman (1984:96).

Limits and Sustainability

Instead of emphasizing that natural resources are limited, Buddhism encourages individuals to limit their resource consumption to the optimal satisfaction of the four basic needs of food, clothing, shelter, and medicine. According to the Middle Way, one lives and progresses in accord with the principles of detachment and moderation (Saddhatissa 1970:74). Detachment from the material and other aspects of the present is essential (Saddhatissa 1970:30). The individual should also simplify needs and devote time to meditation (Saddhatissa 1970:72). In short, the Middle Way avoids the extremes of denial (asceticism) and overindulgence (consumerism) (e.g., de Silva 1987:27–28). It is the "rationed life" in that there is optimal satisfaction of basic needs rather than maximal satisfaction of needs, wants, and desires (Smith 1958:94). Buddhism points to the fundamental distinction between need and greed (Sandell 1987a:35). In such ways Buddhism promotes economic and social sustainability. However, detachment does not mean indifference, as will be discussed later. The Middle Way also points to mediation and accommodation to settle conflicts (Shepard 1990:21).

Diversity

Buddhism advocates reverence and compassion toward all life, including invertebrate and vertebrate animals. Tropical forests are the highest expression of terrestrial biodiversity. Forests are best for meditation because of their natural and peaceful environment (de Silva 1987:21–22). Thus, traditionally temples were often built in forests, and by association the surrounding forest became sacred space to be preserved rather than exploited (Brockelman 1987:97; Buri 1989:53; also see Burkill 1946 and Pei 1985).

Rights

Buddhism emphasizes the intrinsic value of humans and nature (Buri 1989:53; Kabilsingh 1987b:8, 11). This is in contrast to extrinsic value, the economic valuation of nature for resource exploitation for the market, such as in considering forest as board feet of lumber. An individual should only use natural resources to obtain optimal satisfaction of basic needs. "A Buddhist does not sacrifice living beings for worship or food, but sacrifices instead his own selfish motives" (Saddhatissa 1970:88). The Buddhist is more concerned with the contemplation of nature than with its utilitarian use.

Responsibility

The primacy of the mind is the key to Buddhist ethics (Saddhatissa 1970:28). One of the Buddhist texts, the *Dammapada*, begins with the words: "All we are is the result of what we have thought" (Smith 1958:121). From positive thoughts flow positive actions and positive consequences. From negative thoughts flow negative actions and negative consequences. Moreover, the actions of an individual in the present life influence the next one. The source of suffering is in the individual, and likewise the source of happiness is in the individual. Enlightenment derives from the understanding of this reality (Saddhatissa 1970:33). Thus ignorance rather than sin is the problem (Smith 1958:121). Wisdom and morality are mutually reinforcing (Saddhatissa 1970:123–124). Accordingly, Buddhism would encourage the cultivation of environmental education as well as environmental ethics.

These principles are aptly described by Saddhatissa (1970):

> According to the doctrine of karma, future happiness is a direct result or continuation of the maintaining of a satisfactory standard of conduct in the present. But there were wrong actions in the past which must produce their effects in the present and in the future. If inevitably one reaps the results of one's actions, good or bad, and there is no means of avoiding the results on the strength of the moral excellence of another person, the best that can be done to gain secure and lasting well-being is to cut down the evil actions and increase the

good ones (p. 56).

Buddhism recognizing no Deity, there is no being on whose belief the bhikkhu (monk) could act as intermediary with man, either for the performance of ritual or ceremonies, for the asking of favours, or for any other reason. Moreover, no such intervention as the asking for pardon for misdeeds is possible since, automatically, one suffers or enjoys the results of one's actions (p. 82).

As Kaza (1990:25) cogently explains:

The qualities of our thoughts and actions are inextricably linked and have a powerful impact on the environment. It is here that Buddhism can offer a great gift to the world. The root of the environmental crisis lies in the habits of mind as much as the destructive habits of behavior.

Also relevant to responsibility are the first of both the negative and positive precepts which are complementary. The first negative precept is nonviolence, to abstain from taking life. The first positive precept is deep and universal compassion or loving kindness toward all life (Saddhatissa 1970:90; Skolimowski 1990:29). As Saddhatissa (1970:87) explains: "Here the Buddhist undertakes to abstain from destroying, causing to be destroyed, or sanctioning the destruction of a living being. 'Living being' implies anything that has life, from insects up to and including man."

The first negative precept is reinforced by the ideas of karma and rebirth. (Karma refers to the accumulation of good and bad deeds that follow an individual into subsequent rebirths.) Animals may be reborn as humans; humans may be reborn as animals. This rebirth, which also applies to one's self and one's ancestors and relatives, is one good reason for treating animals with kindness and sympathy (de Silva 1987:18–19).

Since nonviolence, the first negative precept, extends to all life, it includes forms such as insects that are not usually identified as a special subject of concern by environmentalists and conservationists. This precept also means that normally Buddhists would not be involved in the kind of violence which is sometimes practiced by radical environmentalists (Manes 1990).

Individual

Since the locus of either happiness or suffering is in the individual, it is up to each individual to cultivate positive thoughts from which will flow positive actions from which will flow positive consequences. This rests on the realization of the Four Noble Truths and the pursuit of the Noble Eightfold Path. It also depends on following the Middle Way of detachment and moderation, satisfying basic needs while avoiding greed. Meditation in nature is an important part of this process of reaching *nirvana,* which is the union with nature through the extinction of self and of all mortal cravings.

ACTIONS AND CONSEQUENCES

If Buddhists followed the preceding ideas of environmental ethics in their actions, then the consequences would probably minimize environmental degradation. As Berry (1987:6) cogently notes:

> The smaller Buddhist countries of South and Southeast Asia, in their pre-modern period, had minimal impact upon the life systems of their regions because of limited populations, village modes of life, and few large urban centers – supported, of course, by a spirituality that exalted a lifestyle detached from earthly possessions.

(See also de Silva 1987:26–27 and Sivaraksa 1985:266.)

As we (Natadecha-Sponsel and Sponsel 1990) have argued on several grounds, most societies in Thailand have apparently been in a *relative* condition of dynamic ecological equilibrium for millennia throughout most of the human prehistory and history of the region. Although severe environmental problems in Thailand have roots that go back at least into the past two centuries when modernization started with Western contact, the environmental crisis, which has eroded biodiversity, did not really develop until after World War II (Hirsch 1988; Hurst 1990:207; Keyes 1983; Moerman and Miller 1989; Reynolds 1976:211, 214).[4] Some basic statistics clearly demonstrate this trend in Thailand. From 1911 to the present the human population increased from a little over 8 million to 52 million. From 1850 to 1984, the area under rice cultivation expanded from 9,000 to 70,000 km².

From 1938 to now, the forest cover decreased from 72 to 18 percent of the country (Sponsel and Natadecha 1988:306–308). The causes of deforestation are multiple, the specific combination varying in time and space, but ultimately the causes are human need and greed (Chunkao 1987; Hurst 1990; Phantumvanit and Sathirathai 1988; Ramitanondh 1989; Sponsel and Natadecha 1988; Sricharatchanya 1987). This tragic reduction of forests and biodiversity occurred in recent decades as Thailand embraced modernization and as there was a correlated weakening of adherence to traditional Buddhism and Thai culture (Reynolds 1976). Indeed, in many respects Western and Buddhist world views and ways are antithetical (Figure 4.1). This

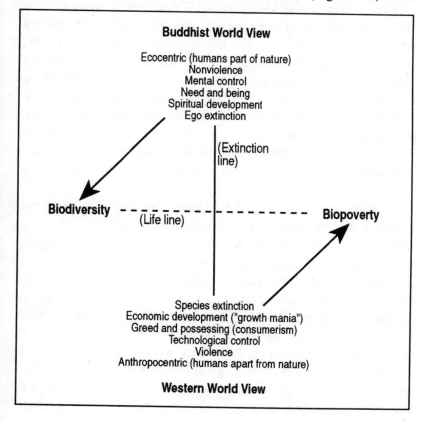

Figure 4.1. World view and biodiversity.

weakening of adherence to tradition in Thailand has been referred to as a "moral collapse" in a benchmark symposium on cultural ecology sponsored by the Siam Society (Kunstadter 1989).

The environmental crisis in Thailand reached its peak through a dramatic catastrophe and public recognition after the disastrous floods of November 1988 in southern Thailand. About 460 people were killed while hundreds remain missing, 70,000 became homeless, and property damage amounted to US$40 million (Hurst 1990:210). The floods were blamed mainly on illegal logging, as thousands of logs washed down hillsides and demolished villages, houses, and bridges. In Lan Saka District, at least one village of 800 homes was completely flattened by logs and flash floods. Part of the response at the governmental level was a ban on logging throughout the country established on January 18, 1989, although its effectiveness is not yet known. This ban has stimulated timber imports from neighboring Mayanmar and Laos, elevating deforestation in those countries (Hurst 1990:212; Lohmann 1989; McCoy-Thompson 1989). Part of the response at the public level was increased environmental activism. Deforestation is now among the central issues in politics in Thailand (Hurst 1990:230). Today in Thailand more than 50 nongovernment organizations are concerned with environmental and conservation issues.

There are many examples of monks leading villagers to put Buddhist ideas into action for conservation purposes. One of the most noteworthy cases is that of the 58-year-old forest monk Pongsak Tejadhammo in the vicinity of Chiang Mai in northern Thailand. He established the Dhammanaat Foundation to conserve remaining forest and to reforest cleared areas to reestablish a greater degree of environmental harmony and security for local villagers. On October 15, 1985, in a historic meeting with villagers from Tambol Mae Soi at Wat Sob Soi, following the Buddhist idea of the interdependence of all things in nature, Pongsak recognized the link between the deterioration of the quality of life and the degradation of the environment through deforestation. He explained how forests function ecologically in the retention of soil and water, cooling the air, promoting rainfall, and so on. He said that the decline of water resources for irrigation, the loss of soil fertility, higher temperatures, and decreased rainfall were all related to deforestation. Accordingly, he advocated protecting the remaining forests and reforesting other areas through community actions based on principles from Buddhism and ecology (Tejadhammo 1985). As a pioneering project in restoration ecology, the monks and the community fenced part of a 70-km^2 area for regeneration with trees and other wildlife of local species. They hope that the regenerated watershed will restore adequate water resources for irrigation at lower elevations (Gray 1987:26). Although sufficient time has not passed to fully assess this experiment, this project in community forest resource management is very promising and may provide a model for similar undertakings elsewhere in the country.

However, there have been some difficulties. For example, the project has created tension and conflict with neighboring Hmong hill tribe villages, which are considered agents of deforestation (Kaye 1990). (Hill tribes are often accused of deforestation even though their cultural ecology, swiddening practices, and corresponding impact on the forest ecosystem are quite varied from group to group [Kunstadter 1988].)[5]

As another example of Buddhist environmentalism, in various areas of Thailand monks have developed a nonviolent strategy of ritually ordaining trees and wrapping them in sacred orange robes, which are usually reserved for clothing monks. For a devout Buddhist in Thailand, it is unpardonable to kill an ordained monk. The symbolism of the sacred robe wrapped around a tree is to deter people from cutting it and thereby helping to preserve it and the surrounding forest.

At an international level, which includes Thailand, also noteworthy is the Buddhist Perception of Nature Project started by Nancy Nash in 1985. The aim of this project is to improve environmental awareness, attitudes, and actions (Kabilsingh 1987b:8; Nash 1987:31). The means is to extract the environmentally relevant material from the vast and rich literature on Buddhism that extends back over 2,500 years. This literature contains vivid stories of monks and lay persons who cut trees or kill animals, parables in which Buddha used nature to illustrate how life should be lived and also the continuity between humans and nature. More than 50,000 copies of environmentally relevant selections from Buddhist scriptures are being distributed to monasteries, colleges, schools, and other institutions in Thailand. Publications of this project include *Tree of Life: Buddhism and Protection of Nature* (Davies 1987) and *A Cry from the Forest* (Kabilsingh 1987a). The project is also developing audiovisual and television programs on the relevance of Buddhism to the environment (Gray 1987:26). This project may eventually provide a model for the development of environmental ethics and environmental education for Buddhist communities elsewhere and a heuristic stimulus for other religions (Meeker 1988).

The most fundamental obstacle to the conservation of forests and biodiversity is the gross discrepancy between ideals and actions (Callicott and Ames 1989a; Buddhadasa 1987:23; Htun 1987:28). It is significant that there has been "a kind of Buddhist revolt against the deterioration of nature," according to Sulak Sivaraksa (Gray 1987:25). The role of Buddhism in environmental ethics, education, and conservation in Thailand has tremendous potential because 95 percent of the people consider themselves Buddhists. Buddhism is the state religion, and there are more than 300,000 monks and 37,000 temples. Joining the monkhood, at least temporarily for a few months or years, is common for males in Thailand, although the practice is not as popular as previously.

CONCLUSIONS

For conserving biodiversity in Thailand, McNeely and Dobias (1991:90) argued that economic incentives can promote greater governmental interest which is decisive, whereas Lohmann (1991) argued that grassroots economic concerns and appropriate actions are more relevant. Lohman (1991:11) asserts that:

> Many grassroots groups tend to have an immediate stake in defending the practices that conserve some level of biodiversity and self-

reliance, while staff of government ministries, international agencies or corporations tend to have a vested interest in encouraging the policies that lead to vicious circles of environmental degradation and impoverishment.

Although these materialist considerations are certainly important, in our opinion so are mentalist ones (i.e., Buddhist ideals and actions).

Bodhi (1987:vii) most appropriately summarizes the relevance of Buddhism for the development of an environmental ethic:

> With its philosophic insight into the interconnectedness and thoroughgoing interdependence of all conditioned things, with its thesis that happiness is to be found through the restraint of desire in a life of contentment rather than through the proliferation of desire, with its goal of enlightenment through renunciation and contemplation and its ethic of non-injury and boundless loving-kindness for all beings, Buddhism provides all the essential elements for a relationship to the natural world characterized by respect, care and compassion.

Clearly, environmental ethics inherent in Buddhism are relevant for conserving biodiversity, especially in Southeast and East Asian countries. The greatest obstacle is the lack of adherence to ideals in practice. But there appears to be a revitalization movement developing in Thailand in reaction to the environmental crisis as well as the stresses and problems of modernization in general – a movement to strengthen traditions of Buddhism and culture and to restore a greater measure of ecological equilibrium. Perhaps the most vital question, which remains to be answered in the future, is whether there will be enough effective action in time to avoid even graver environmental and social crises in Thailand.

NOTES

1. For discussions of the relationship between religion and ecology in general, see Berry 1987, Dwivedi 1988, Hultkrantz 1987, and Rappaport 1979.
2. Alyanak 1991, Badiner 1990, Barash 1973, Berry 1987, Bloom 1972, Buddhadasa 1987, Burkill 1946, Calderazzo 1991, Callicott and Ames

1989b, Capra 1975, Darlington 1990, Davies 1987, Galtung 1988, Gray 1987, Kabilsingh 1987a, Kaza 1990, Keyes 1983, Natadecha 1988, Ophuls 1977, Pei 1985, Randhawa 1965, Robinson 1972, Sandell 1987b, Schumacher 1973, Shepard 1990, Skolimowski 1990, Sponsel and Natadecha 1988, Thick Nhat Hanh 1988, Thurman 1984, WWFI 1986.

3. Among the surveys of Buddhist ethics, especially useful are Saddhatissa (1970) and Tachibana (1926).

4. Thailand is part of a transitional zone between moist (evergreen) and dry (deciduous or seasonal) forests (Myers 1984:42). There are several different subtypes of forest in Thailand, depending on altitude, climate, soils, and other factors: lowland evergreen, hill evergreen, coniferous, mixed deciduous, dipterocarp, mangrove, and so on (Chunkao 1987; Myers 1984:104-106; Sternstein 1976:35-40). As part of a transitional zone among three major biogeographical realms, Thailand has 870 avian species and 263 mammalian species, including 94 bat species (Hurst 1990:210).

5. See Darlington 1990 for a detailed study of monks as environmental activists in northern Thailand.

REFERENCES

Alyanak, Leyla. 1991. "Man and Nature: The Zen Buddhists of Brazil." *The New Road* 17:1, 4–6.

Badiner, Allan Hunt, ed. 1990. *Dharma Gaia: A Harvest of Essays in Buddhism and Ecology*. Berkeley, CA: Parallax Press.

Barash, D. P. 1973. "The Ecologist As Zen Master." *American Midland Naturalist* 89:214–217.

Berry, Thomas. 1987. "Religions, Ecology, and Economics." *Breakthrough* 8(1–2): 4–11.

Bloom, Alfred. 1972. "Buddhism, Nature, and Environment." *The Eastern Buddhist* 5(1): 115–129.

Bodhi, Bhikkhu. 1987. "Foreword," in Klas Sandell, ed., *Buddhist Perspectives on the Ecocrisis*. Pp. v–viii. Kandy, Sri Lanka: Buddhist Publication Society.

Britannica Book of the Year 1990. Chicago: Encyclopaedia Britannica, Inc.

Brockelman, Warren. 1987. "Nature Conservation," in Anat Arbhabhirama, Dhira Phantumvanit, John Elkington, and Phaitoon Ingkasuwan, eds., *Thailand Natural Resources Profile*. Pp. 90–119. Bangkok: Thailand Development Research Institute.

Buddhadasa, Bhikkhu. 1987. "A Notion of Buddhist Ecology." *Seeds of Peace* 3(2): 22–27.

Buri, Rachit. 1989. "Wildlife in Thai Culture," in *Culture and Environment in Thailand*. Pp. 51–59. Bangkok: Siam Society.

Burkill, I. H. 1946. "On the Dispersal of the Plants Most Intimate to Buddhism." *Journal of the Arnold Arboretum* 27(4): 327–339.

Calderazzo, John. 1991. "Meditation in a Thai Forest." *Audubon* Jan/Feb 1991:84–91.

Callicott, J. Baird, and Roger T. Ames. 1989a. "Epilogue: On the Relation of Idea and Action," in J. Baird Callicott and Roger T. Ames, eds., *Nature in Asian Traditions of Thought: Essays on Environmental Philosophy*. Pp. 279–289. Albany, NY: State University of New York Press.

Callicott, J. Baird, and Roger T. Ames, eds. 1989b. *Nature in Asian Traditions of Thought: Essays on Environmental Philosophy*. Albany, NY: State University of New York Press.

Capra, Fritjof. 1975. *The Tao of Physics*. New York: Bantam Books.

Capra, Fritjof. 1980. "Buddhist Physics," in Satish Kumar, ed., *The Schumacher Lectures*. Pp. 121–143. New York: Harper and Row.

Chunkao, Kasem. 1987. "Forest Resources," in Anat Arbhabhirama, Dhira Phantumvanit, John Elkington, and Phaitoon Ingkasuwan, eds., *Thailand: Natural Resources Profile*. Pp. 73–88. Bangkok: Thailand Development Research Institute.

Darlington, Susan Marie. 1990. Buddhism, Morality and Change: The Local Response to Development in Northern Thailand. Doctoral dissertation, University of Michigan, Ann Arbor.

Davies, Shann, ed. 1987. *Tree of Life: Buddhism and Protection of Nature*. Hong Kong: Buddhist Perception of Nature Project.

de Silva, Lily. 1987. "The Buddhist Attitude Towards Nature," in Klas Sandell, ed., *Buddhist Perspectives on the Ecocrisis*. Pp. 9–29. Kandy, Sri Lanka: Buddhist Publication Society.

Dwivedi, O. P. 1988. "Man and Nature: An Holistic Approach to a Theory of Ecology." *The Environmental Professional* 10:8–15.

Ehrlich, Paul. 1988. "The Loss of Diversity: Causes and Consequences," in E. O. Wilson, ed., *Biodiversity*. Pp. 21–27. Washington, DC: National Academy Press.

Galtung, Johan. 1988. *Buddhism: A Quest for Unity and Peace*. Honolulu, HI: Dae Won Sa Buddhist Temple of Hawai'i.

Goldsmith, Edward, ed. 1988. "Special 'Deep Ecology' Issue." *The Ecologist* 18(4/5).

Gray, Dennis D. 1987. "Buddhism Being Used to Help Save Asia's Environment." *Seeds of Peace* 3(2): 24–26.

Hirsh, Phillip. 1988. "Spontaneous Land Settlement and Deforestation in

Thailand," in John Dargavel, Kay Dixon, and Noel Semple, eds., *Changing Tropical Forests: Historical Perspectives on Today's Challenges in Asia, Australasia and Oceania*. Pp. 359–376. Canberra, Australia: Centre for Resource and Environmental Studies.

Htun, Nay. 1987. "The State of the Environment Today: The Needs for Tomorrow," in Shann Davies, ed., *Tree of Life: Buddhism and Protection of Nature*. Pp. 19–29. Hong Kong: Buddhist Perception of Nature Project.

Hultkrantz, Ake. 1987. "Ecology," in *The Encyclopedia of Religion* 4:581–585.

Hurst, Philip. 1990. "Thailand," in *Rainforest Politics: Ecological Destruction in South-East Asia*. Pp. 207–244. Atlantic Highlands, NJ: Zed Books.

Kabilsingh, Chatsumarn. 1987a. *A Cry from the Forest: Buddhist Perception of Nature: A New Perspective for Conservation Education*. Bangkok: Wildlife Fund, Thailand.

Kabilsingh, Chatsumarn. 1987b. "How Buddhism Can Help Protect Nature," in Shann Davies, ed., *Tree of Life: Buddhism and Protection of Nature*. Pp. 7–16. Hong Kong: Buddhist Perception of Nature Project.

Kaye, Lincoln. 1990. "Of Cabbages and Cultures: Buddhist 'Greens' Aim to Oust Thailand's Hilltribes." *Far Eastern Economic Review* (December 13): 35–37.

Kaza, Stephanie. 1990. "Towards a Buddhist Environmental Ethic." *Buddhism at the Crossroads* (Fall): 22–25.

Keyes, Charles F. 1983. "Economic Action and Buddhist Morality in a Thai Village." *Journal of Asian Studies* 42(4): 851–868.

Komin, Suntaree. 1985. "The World View Through Thai Value Systems," in *Traditional and Changing Thai World View*. Pp. 170–192. Bangkok: Chulalongkorn University Social Research Institute.

Kunstadter, Peter. 1988. "Hill People of Northern Thailand," in Julie Sloan Denslow and Christine Padoch, eds., *People of the Tropical Rain Forest*. Pp. 93–110. Berkeley, CA: University of California Press.

Kunstadter, Peter. 1989. "The End of the Frontier: Culture and Environment Interactions in Thailand," in *Culture and Environment in Thailand*. Pp. 543–552. Bangkok: Siam Society.

Lester, Robert C. 1987. *Buddhism*. San Francisco, CA: Harper and Row.

Lohmann, Larry. 1989. "Forestry in Thailand: The Logging Ban and Its Consequences." *Seeds of Peace* 5(3): 17–19.

Lohmann, Larry. 1991. "Who Defends Biological Diversity? Conservation Strategies and the Case of Thailand." *The Ecologist* 21(1): 5–13.

Manes, Christopher. 1990. *Green Rage: Radical Environmentalism and the Unmaking of Civilization.* Boston: Little, Brown.

McCoy-Thompson, Meri. 1989. "Sliding Slopes Break Thai Logjam." *World Watch* 2(5): 8–9.

McNeely, Jeffrey A., and Robert J. Dobias. 1991. "Economic Incentives for Conserving Biodiversity in Thailand." *Ambio* 20(2): 86–90.

McNeely, Jeffrey A., Kenton R. Miller, Walter V. Reid, Russell A. Mittermeier, and Timothy B. Werner. 1990. *Conserving the World's Biological Diversity.* IUCN, Gland, Switzerland; WRI, CI, WWF-US, and the World Bank, Washington, DC.

Meeker, Joseph W. 1988. "The Assisi Connection." *Wilderness* 51(180): 61–63.

Moerman, Michael, and Patricia L. Miller. 1989. "Changes in a Village's Relations with Its Environment," in *Culture and Environment in Thailand.* Pp. 303–326. Bangkok: Siam Society.

Monk, Robert C., Walter C. Hofheinz, Kenneth T. Lawrence, Joseph D. Stamey, Bert Affleck, and Tetsunao Yamamori. 1987. *Exploring Religious Meaning*, 3rd edn. Englewood Cliffs, NJ: Prentice-Hall.

Myers, Norman. 1984. *The Primary Source: Tropical Forests and Our Future.* NY: W. W. Norton.

Nash, Nancy. 1987. "The Buddhist Perception of Nature Project," in Shann Davies, ed., *Tree of Life: Buddhism and Protection of Nature.* Pp. 31–33. Hong Kong: Buddhist Perception of Nature Project.

Natadecha, Poranee. 1988. "Buddhist Religion and Scientific Ecology as Convergent Conceptions of Nature," in Diana MacIntyre DeLuca, ed., *Essays on Perceiving Nature.* Pp. 113–118. Honolulu, HI: Perceiving Nature Conference Committee.

Natadecha-Sponsel, Poranee, and Leslie E. Sponsel. 1990. The Ecological Transition and Buddhism in Relation to Forests and Deforestation in Thailand. Paper presented at the Third Annual Conference of the Northwest Regional Consortium for Southeast Asian Studies, 19–21 October, Seattle, Washington.

Ophuls, William. 1977. "Buddhist Politics." *The Ecologist* 7(3): 82–86.

Pei, Shengji. 1985. "Some Effects of the Dai People's Cultural Beliefs and Practices on the Plant Environment of Xishuangbanna, Yunnan Province, Southwest China," in Karl L. Hutterer, A. Terry Rambo, and George Lovelace, eds., *Cultural Values and Human Ecology in Southeast Asia.* Pp. 321–339. Paper No. 27. Ann Arbor: University of Michigan.

Phantumvanit, Dhira, and Khunying Suthawan Sathirathai. 1988. "Thailand: Degradation and Development in a Resource-Rich Land." *Environment*

30(1): 10–15.

Rajavaramuni, Phra. 1985. *Thai Buddhism in the Buddhist World: A Survey of the Buddhist Situation Against a Historical Background*. Bangkok, Thailand: Mahachulaklongkorn Buddhist University Wat Mahadhatu.

Ramitanondh, Shalardchai. 1989. "Forests and Deforestation in Thailand: A Pandisciplinary Approach," in *Culture and Environment in Thailand*. Pp. 23–50. Bangkok: Siam Society.

Randhawa, M. S. 1965. *The Cult of Trees and Tree-Worship in Buddhist-Hindu Scripture*. New Delhi, India: All India Fine Arts and Crafts Society.

Rappaport, Roy A. 1979. *Ecology, Meaning, and Religion*. Richmond, CA: North Atlantic Books.

Reynolds, Craig J. 1976. "Buddhist Cosmography in Thai History, with Special Reference to Nineteenth-Century Culture Change." *Journal of Asian Studies* 35(2): 203–220.

Robinson, Peter. 1972. "Some Thoughts on Buddhism and the Ethics of Ecology." *Proceedings of the New Mexico–West Texas Philosophical Society* (Albuquerque) 7:71–78.

Saddhatissa, H. 1970. *Buddhist Ethics*. NY: G. Braziller.

Sandell, Klas. 1987a. "Buddhist Philosophy As Inspiration to Ecodevelopment," in Klas Sandell, ed., *Buddhist Perspectives on the Ecocrisis*. Pp. 30–37. Kandy, Sri Lanka: Buddhist Publication Society.

Sandell, Klas, ed. 1987b. *Buddhist Perspectives on the Ecocrisis*. Kandy, Sri Lanka: Buddhist Publication Society.

Schumacher, E. F. 1973. *Small Is Beautiful: Economics As If People Mattered*. NY: Harper and Row.

Shepard, Philip T. 1990. "Turning On to the Environment Without Turning Off Other People." *Buddhism at the Crossroads* (Fall): 18–21.

Shrader-Frechette, K. S. 1981. *Environmental Ethics*. Pacific Grove, CA: Boxwood Press.

Sivaraksa, Sulak. 1985. "Rural Poverty and Development in Thailand, Indonesia, and the Philippines." *The Ecologist* 15(5/6): 266–268.

Skolimowski, Henry K. 1981. *Eco-Philosophy: Designing New Tactics for Living*. Boston: M. Boyars.

Skolimowski, Henry K. 1990. "Eco-Philosophy and Buddhism." *Buddhism at the Crossroads* (Fall): 26–29.

Smith, Huston. 1958. "Buddhism," in *The Religions of Man*. Pp. 90–159. NY: Harper and Row.

Sponsel, Leslie E., and Poranee Natadecha. 1988. "Buddhism, Ecology, and Forests in Thailand: Past, Present, and Future," in John Dargavel, Kay

Dixon, and Noel Semple, eds., *Changing Tropical Forests: Historical Perspectives on Today's Challenges in Asia, Australasia, and Oceania.* Pp. 305–325. Canberra, Australia: Centre for Resource and Environmental Studies.

Sricharatchanya, Paisal. 1987. "Jungle Warfare: Thailand Mounts Campaign to Save Its Trees." *Far Eastern Economic Review* (September 17): 86–88.

Sternstein, Larry. 1976. *Thailand: The Environment of Modernization.* NY: McGraw-Hill.

Tachibana, Shundo. 1926. *The Ethics of Buddhism.* New York: Barnes and Noble.

Tejadhammo, Pongsak. 1985. "A Talk by Abbot Pongsak Tejadhammo of Wat Palad and Wat Tam Tu Poo given at a meeting of villagers in Wat Sob Soi in Tambol Mae Soi, Amphur Jomtong, Chiang Mai Province, on October 15, 1985," Chiang Mai, Thailand.

Thick Nhat Hanh. 1988. "The Individual, Society, and Nature," in Fred Eppsteiner, ed., *The Path of Compassion: Writings on Socially Engaged Buddhism.* Berkeley, CA: Parallax Press.

Thurman, Robert A. F. 1984. "Buddhist Views of Nature: Variations on the Theme of Mother-Father Harmony," in Leroy S. Rounder, ed., *On Nature.* Pp. 96–112. Notre Dame, IN: University of Notre Dame Press.

Wilson, E. O., ed. 1988. *Biodiversity.* Washington, DC: National Academy Press.

WWFI (World Wildlife Fund International). 1986. *The Assisi Declarations: Messages on Man and Nature from Buddhism, Christianity, Hinduism, Islam, and Judaism.* Washington, DC: World Wildlife Fund.

Chapter 5

The Religious and Ethical Tradition of Ancient and Contemporary Australia: Its Role in the Setting of Modern Goals

Ranil Senanayake

Landscape Introduction

To appreciate the human traditions of a land, it is pertinent to understand the history of that landscape. The traditions of ancient Australia are so interlocked with the land that they provide the best human response to ensure ecosystem sustainability. However, contemporary humans have changed the ecological relations of the landscape so radically that a new approach will be required to ensure landscape stability. Modern landscape management may require a different paradigm; it may require a different ethic.

To manage a landscape, it is important to understand its ecological history (R. L. Clark 1990). The landscapes of Australia, though diverse and species rich, share some vital common characteristics. The landforms are old. The prominent soil features have been worked and re-worked to present the relatively homogeneous soil landscapes of the current continental landmass (Stephens 1961). Except for the eastern seaboard, the climate changes throughout the continent are smooth and gradual, rarely abrupt. Within these broad climatic belts, strong localized differences in rainfall exist for relatively short periods. Further, rainfall through much of this area occurs as episodic events, as unpredictable storms rather than regular showers (Leeper 1970). These features have produced a vegetation that is homogeneous phytogeographically (Doing 1981), but displaying very strong localized elements. The eastern seaboard, with its complex landscapes and high rainfall, became the refuge for the remnant patches of rainforest containing species of Gondwanaic orgins (Walker and Singh 1981) and contains greater phytogeographical complexity.

ABORIGINAL LANDSCAPE MANAGEMENT

A similar pattern is suggested in human grouping. The hypothesis that human social organization had boundary conditions that were contiguous with functional landscape boundaries has been made clear by studies of tribal boundaries (Tindale 1974; I.D. Clark 1990:364–365). Figure 5.1 illustrates social boundaries at a linguistic level that are correlated with landscape boundaries at a watershed level. This homogeneity in general, with strong localized elements, is also demonstrated at a religious level. Central to all Aboriginal religious tradition is the "Dreaming." This complex, pluralistic term has a number of distinct though connected meanings and has been summarized thus by Charlesworth (1984).

- It is a narrative, mythical account of the foundation and shaping of the entire world by the ancestor heroes who are uncreated and eternal.

- It refers to the embodiment of the spiritual power of the ancestor heroes in the land in certain sites, in species of fauna and flora, so that its power is available to people today making the land itself a religious icon.

- It denotes the general way of life or "Law" (e.g., moral and social precepts, rituals, ceremonial practices).

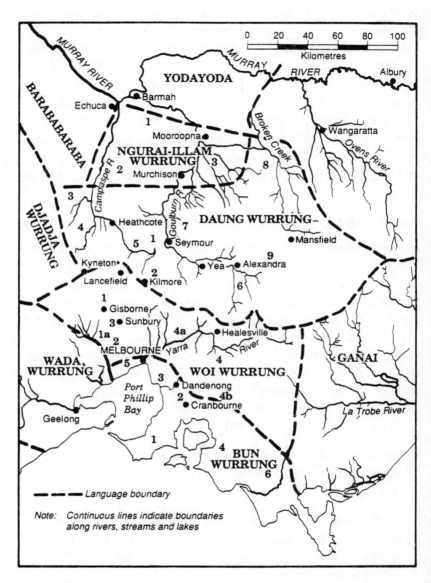

Figure 5.1. Language areas and clans around Melbourne, Victoria.
Reprinted, by permission of the author and Monash University,
Australia, from I. D. Clark, 1990:364–365.

Bun wurrung clans

1. Bun wurrung balug — Point Nepean and Cape Schank
2. Mayune balug — Carrum Swamp, "Mayune" station
3. Ngaruk willam — Brighton, Mordialloc, Dandenong, & between Mts. Eliza & Martha
4. Yallock balug — Bass River, Tooradin
5. Yalukit willam — East of Werribee River, Williamstown, Sandridge & St. Kilda
6. Yowengarra — Tarwin River

Daung wurrung clans

1. Buthera balug — Goulburn River, about Seymour
2. Look willam — Campaspe River, near Kilmore
3. Moomoom gundidj — West of Campaspe River, and northwest of Mitchellstown
4. Nattarak balug — Coliban River and Upper Campaspe River
5. Nira balug — Kilmore, Broadford, and Pyalong
6. Warring-illam balug — Yea
7. Yarran-illam balug — Mitchellstown
8. Yeerun-illam balug — Benalla
9. Yowung-illam balug — Alexandra

Ngurai-illam wurrung clans

1. Benbedora balug — Elmore
2. Gunung willam — Campaspe River
3. Ngurai-illam balug — Murchison

Woi wurrung clans

1. Gunung willam balug — Mt. Macedon
1a. Tallin willam — Toolern Creek
2. Kurung jang balug — Werribee River and Mt. Cottrell
3. Marin balug — Kororoit Creek
4. Wurrundjeri balug — Yarra River
4a. Wurrundjeri willam — Yarra River
4b. Bulug willam — Kooweerup Swamp

Key to numbering, by clan name and approximate location, for Figure 5.1

- It refers to the personal identity or vocation that individuals may have by virtue of their clan or spirit conception relating them to particular sites.

Even the myth has a consistent pantheon, The Rainbow Serpent, as creator spirit (Porter 1990): the "All Father" figure represented under a variety of names such as *Baiame, Bunjil, Daramulen, Nurelli* (Oldmeadow 1990), or the "All Mother" figure of the northern tribes (Maddock 1984).

An equally ubiquitous life strategy was seen throughout the continent. Agriculture or animal husbandry was minimal; hunting and gathering was the practiced lifestyle. Although there is evidence of aquaculture at certain historical sites (Coutts et al. 1978), the dominant technology has been the use of the fire stick and digging stick. The use of fire as a hunting or management tool shaped much of their landscape and may have determined the pre-European vegetation patterns (Walker and Singh 1981).

The arrival of humans in Australia has been recorded at over 30–40,000 B.P. (Bowler 1976; Thorne 1981). Pollen and sediment studies suggest that this landscape may have supported a very different flora to that experienced by the first European settlers. For instance, the distribution of fire-sensitive taxa (*Auracaria, Podocarpus, Cyathea*) was greater at about 50–60,000 B.P., although the relative dominance of fire-sensitive or fire-adapted species depended on changes in climatic events (Walker and Singh 1981). The incidence of greatest fire activity and consequently the assertion of sclerophyll woodland is seen to be contemporaneous with the arrival of humans and has been attributed to human actions (Singh et al. 1980; Kershaw 1986). Although climate remained the major determinant of vegetation distribution or change (R. L. Clark 1983), Aboriginal land use, particularly burning, could affect the rate of change by reinforcing or opposing the climatically determined direction of change (Mcphail 1980). Thus, humans have been identified as agents in determining the vegetation complex for many thousands of years, so that many landscapes encountered by the first Europeans were "cultural" landscapes (R. L. Clark 1990).

The mythologically based tradition that evolved within society over this time possessed an array of religious practices. These were spatially oriented rather than temporally oriented and embedded in a ritual-ceremonial complex centering on a sacramental relationship with the land itself (Oldmeadow 1990). People received their identity within the totemic system: their authority, position, social prestige, and relationships from the area in which they were born or conceived (Strehlow 1964). This produced a love for the land that was not only an emotional response but even more in the sense that an individual and his or her soul were indivisibly tied to it in a physical and spiritual unity (Rudder 1978). This concern is always voiced when there is a perceived threat to the land. Davis (1983) records traditional custodians commenting, "We are worried. We need our land. We want it to stay spotless. We don't want to see a tree cut down." Such observations are common in this document. To Aboriginal people, the land has a vital life-giving importance. As with many traditional people, land is not perceived as a tradeable commodity. It provides the sense of the sacred that has been used to identify "civilization" (Schuon 1976; Coomaraswamy 1979). They have a special relationship with the land, and that relationship is dynamic, requiring an ongoing commitment to maintenance and care (Downing 1988). These observations suggest a highly co-evolved ecosystem driven by humans – an ecosystem whose management is determined by the human information maintained within the local community. Their experiences are interpreted and expressed through a body of traditional ecological knowledge (Bains 1986).

An example of the working of such an environmentally sensitive management system emerges from research with the Martu of the Great and Little Sandy deserts of Western Australia. The Martu had a detailed vocabulary for various types of rain, cloud, wind, and other weather phenomena (Tonkinson 1978). The biotic responses to these were identified with "sub-seasons." The seasonal response of various landscape elements such as dune or rocky land was identified by indicators peculiar to those systems. The responses or indicators that were used varied from the color of the grass, to the calling of a cricket, a species of plant, or the nesting of a bird (Walsh 1990). As a result, the ancient ecosystem management information developed a calendar that was responsive to biotic events in preference to abiotic events. This information set contained a knowledge of the celestial measurement system but placed more emphasis on the biotic expression of "season." This ecological knowledge, contained in language and perception, is well documented in Walsh (1990). On a landscape scale, fire is the most significant factor in determining the biotic component of many systems managed by humans (Figure 5.2). The use of fire to promote the regeneration of preferred resource species may have increased the diversity of habitats to form a patch mosaic (Latz and Griffin 1978). In other management strategies, measures were taken to enhance the productivity of certain food species by spreading seed or propagules (Kimber 1984). The evidence that Aboriginal knowledge has tremendous utility in land management is being recognized today. However, the evidence that this method of land management requires an ethical and personal relationship with the land is still poorly appreciated.

EUROPEAN APPROACH TO THE LANDSCAPE

Contemporary Australia has a much shorter history, just 200 years old. In this time the landscape has changed in a dramatic manner. The transposition of European civilization with its attendant patterns of land use has been described an an "apocalyptic event for Australian ecosystems" (Adamson and Fox 1982). Modern ecological science is beginning to appreciate the degree of the calamity as stated by Lowenthal (1976): "Nowhere else had technological man lately occupied so fragile an ecosystem; nowhere else had settlers so utterly failed to identify with their new landscapes; nowhere else was man's environmental impact so patently reprehensible." The early efforts at providing for the spiritual aspect of contemporary civilization seem to have been just as misdirected. To quote Porter (1990): "In the coming century, however, the churches would pay the price of the failures of

A. Species richness of food plants that occurred on major landform units. Mean and standard error.

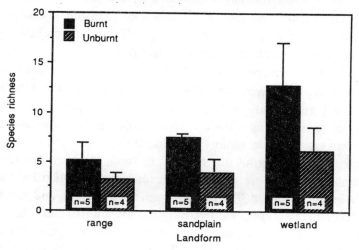

B. Diversity indices of food plants that occurred on major landform units. Mean and standard error.

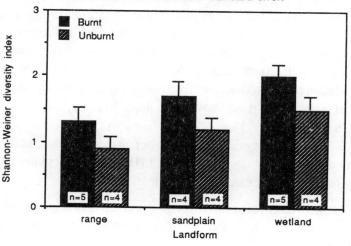

Figure 5.2. Effects of burning.
Source: Walsh 1990. Reprinted by permission of the publisher.

the nineteenth century. The failures – to attract or serve the needs of the working class, to adapt a European style of ministry to a vastly different climate and terrain, to incarnate Christian theology in Australian experience, to overcome the hostilities and prejudices of the old world – would all extract a heavy penalty."

The initial response of the first waves of contemporary immigrants to Australia was to emulate England, its hedges and its fruit trees and green and pleasant fields, to the exclusion of almost everything Australian (Blainey 1980). Alien plants, animals, and agroecosystems were rapidly introduced. The spread of the new species was so vigorous that Hooker, in 1860, observed that native species of plants were replaced by exotic species when land was disturbed or modified. The rapid growth in agriculture and industry has resulted in a corresponding loss or modification of native ecosystems, but the cost of poor ecological land management became evident in a relatively short period. The national cost of droughts, dust storms, and massive erosion is significant in modern history (Beckermann and Coventry 1987). The state of agricultural soil provides an illustration of this cost. The most recent national assessment published in 1978 (CSCS) serves as the principal authority on the poor state of Australian soils. The results of the study showed 51 percent of agricultural land needed treatment. The mechanisms of degradation considered were water erosion, wind erosion, salinization, loss of vegetation, mass movement, frost heaving, and tunneling (CSCS 1978).

The relative intensity of this impact on the native landscape has been categorized by degree of impact (Hobbs and Hopkins 1990). They recognize four categories.

1. Complete removal of the vegetation and disruption of ecological processes, such as occurs during urban development or mining.

2. Removal of vegetation and replacement with intensively managed systems such as agriculture or plantation forestry.

3. Utilization of existing vegetation with some consequent modification, as in pastoralism and timber harvesting in native
forests.

4. Conservation with minimum modification.

Their study of the percentage of the total land area of Australia
devoted to each major land use categorized in the foregoing manner
(Table 5.1) suggests that the major part of the landmass is devoted to
contemporary management systems. The consequences of contemporary and Aboriginal management of land is evident in the recent
landsat images of the Northern Territory where large cattle-grazing

1. Complete vegetation removal	
Mining	< 0.1
Urban	0.1
Transport	1.2
2. Replacement with agricultural systems	
Intensive cropping	0.3
Extensive cropping	5.8
3. Exploitation of native vegetation	
Forestry	2.0
Nonarid grazing	17.4
Arid grazing	43.7
4. No deliberate modification	
Unused (mainly desert)	26.0
Nature conservation	3.5

Table 5.1. Total land area of Australia devoted to each major land
use, categorized by degree of modification of native vegetation (in
percentages).
Source: Hobbs and Hopkins 1990. Reprinted by permission of the
publisher.

properties abut Aboriginal land. The massive erosion damage wrought by contemporary land managers contrast starkly with the stable landscapes of the Aboriginal land (Landsat 1989). Perhaps it is a consequence of the fact that "The trauma of failure ... does not affect the White man who goes away saying that he did his best, but it has a profound effect on Aborigines who have to stay and contend with the compounding strain and tension" (Wallace and Wallace 1977).

RELIGIOUS TRADITIONS AND ENVIRONMENT

The religious tradition of ancient Australia has served well and has the potential to guide future management of native land. What of contemporary Australia? The religious tradition of contemporary Australia was Judeo-Christian and functioned under the assumption that Christianity and European civilization were inseparable (Porter 1990). Further, the first representation of the church to the new land was a young parson who was answerable to the civil and military authorities "according to the rules and disciplines of war" (Bollen 1973). Thus, the church was directed by the administration. As a result the antipathy toward the church was such that the first house of worship constructed in 1793 was burned to the ground by arsonists in 1795. In addition, the utter disregard for indigenous people and their religion can be appreciated by the perception of representatives from the church of England toward other Christian institutions. The Catholic Irish were seen as "a savage race ... destitute of every principle of religion and morality" (Porter 1990; Hogan 1987). Around 1830, the plurality of denominational orders began to flourish and develop. Today, more than 60 percent of Australians say that they pray, meditate, or contemplate at least occasionally. However, only about 25 percent attend formal worship. Religion is widely seen as a matter of private, individual piety. To quote Porter (1990), "While institutional religion is not attractive to most Australians, and some even find it alienating, they are not godless ... many Australians seek an active relationship with God, though not through the churches."

The evolution of contemporary Christian tradition, with its stress on the instrumental value of nonhuman forms of life, has either ignored or denied any value of nature in itself (White 1967). These habits of thought have been seen to be partly responsible for environmental problems in the West and regions that have become Westernized (Bratton 1984). With such a past, it is not surprising that the ecosystems of the new land were doomed to suffer in the manner described earlier. The emergence of a modern theological world view termed "process theology" (Cobb and Griffin 1976), requiring an intuitive and sympathetic apprehension of other creatures (McDaniel 1986), heralded the possibility for fundamental shift in attitudes toward the land.

NEW ATTITUDES AND NEW LANDSCAPE ECOLOGY INSIGHTS

Australian philosophers began to point out that attitudes toward land had to alter significantly if a change in contemporary land management was to be brought about (Robert 1984). These attitude shifts are now becoming apparent in modern Australian society (Hobbs and Hopkins 1990) and are exemplified by calls for:

- involvement of Aboriginal information in nature conservation and land management (Kean et al. 1988);

- use of "sustainable wisdom" in farming (Campbell 1989);

- response to revegetation programs on an individual, group, community, and state level (Burke and Youl 1990); or

- landcare program at a national level (NSCP, in press).

The initial response to landcare has been a massive tree-planting program. Questions still remain important issues for the setting of contemporary goals, including what patterns will this type of response produce on the landscape, and how responsive will they be to long-term needs?

These questions are especially pertinent when the radical difference between form and function between the pleisoclimatic or natural, and anthropomorphic or human-modified elements of the landscape are considered. The natural ecoystems possess more woody vegetation, more perennials, a higher species diversity, and different soil ecosystems (Senanayake 1990). The haphazard replacement of one with the other has brought about the plethora of problems discussed earlier. A good example can be drawn from the increase in dryland salinity, created by clearing large amounts of native forests for pasture establishment, in areas where a rise in the groundwater level meant an upwicking of salt. The native forests arrested this rise in groundwater level by the active evapotranspiration of rainfall. When the trees were removed and replaced with shallow-rooted pasture, the rainwater acted to recharge and raise the level of groundwater with disastrous results (Figures 5.3A and B). However, there are also examples of weed species providing unintended benefits. An example is the role of the highly invasive exotic shrub *Ullex europaeus* (gorse) in providing essential habitat to the endangered and restricted Eastern Barred Bandicoot (*Perameles gunnii*) in Victoria (Brown 1987). Understanding the impact of the new landscape elements and designing them to meet modern goals is the challenge.

A systematic understanding of a landscape is essential to this endeavor. The work on *Landscape Ecology* (Foreman and Godron 1986) suggests many ways of perceiving the landscape in planning processes and provides useful definitions. But, as observed by Rackham (1991), there are fashions in land use that tend to generate fashions in landscape. However, because these landscapes depend on the growth of trees and other long-lived plants, they can never catch up with a fashion before it changes. The new landscapes of 1970, for instance, are no longer new in 1990, but we are saddled with them for the rest of our lives (Rackham 1991). This consideration in landscape planning should involve resistance to fashion and concentrate more on meaning.

In Australia, the ancient traditions suggest how we may interpret such meaning. The land was an entity and communicated its

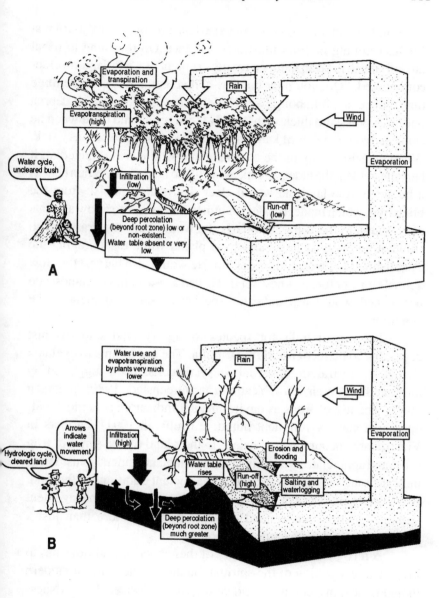

Figure 5.3. Groundwater cycle on (A) uncleared land; (B) cleared land

status to the human observer. An experience recounted by journalist Michael Leunig in 1988 illustrates this fact. On returning to tribal lands that had to be abandoned for government use, a Pitjanjarra elder commented, "Oh, you poor bugger." The comment was made three times: once at a billabong (waterhole) that was choked with debris, once in a grassland thick with *Acacia* thorn scrub, and once when he came across a number of kangaroos – some of which were very sick. When questioned about the comment and who it was directed at, it became evident the elder was speaking to the landscape. When he was a hunter on the land, he would clear debris and rubbish from the billabong, which made it easier for him to hunt and also allow animals easy access to the water. Similarly, he would burn the grassland to stimulate growth of grass and food plants while discouraging the establishment of woody, thorn scrub. He would also harvest the slow animals long before sickness set in. He had an awareness of landscape health and would use indicator species or states to identify the condition.

The use of indicator species to signify land status is just beginning to be recognized in Australia. The use of ants to evaluate change in Australian terrestrial ecosystems has been suggested by many authors (Weir 1978; Yeatman and Greenslade 1980; Andersen 1990). The use of frogs as environmental indicators is being developed as a state government initiative (Sullivan 1991). Farmers in Victoria are encouraged to "listen" to their land (in the sense of frog calls) and appreciate its meaning in terms of management goals. These indicators are very much an echo of the ancient traditions of the land. However, to make use of this type of information in land management requires a will to understand the land as being more than just a commodity for the generation of money.

A recognition of the validity of these ancient traditions has to involve a recognition of the spiritual quality of the land. In modern thought, the transpersonal world view termed "deep ecology" (Naess 1989) seeks an extension of self, with the rest of nature including trees, ecosystems, and the biosphere as a whole. This, together with the postmodern ecological world view (Birch 1990) that finds intrinsic value in all individual entities, from protons to people, provides a basis for reconciling the long perceived dichotomy between humanity and the rest of nature. The need to accept the spiritual quality of the environment is underscored by Tillich (1967) who states, "We come from nature. If God had nothing to do with nature, he finally has nothing to do with our total being because we are nature." Further, modern philosophers (e.g., Cochran 1972) point out that nature cannot be divided into life and non-life, that they are merely positions on a scale graduated from simple (non-life) to complex (life). This position is consistent with other philosophical viewpoints. Farrer (1908) states, "For all forms of life are one; there is no essential difference between the life of a rock and the life of a man – no real difference in kind, though an incalculably vast difference in degree; yet it is the same spirit that possesses both. And all creation, from man down to the lowest animalcule and grain of dust, is moving steadily, if slowly, upward on a vast ascending spiral ... into the prefect of pure Buddha," or as Whitehead (1978) states, "God is not before all creation, but with all creation." Here lies the common element in spiritual tradition that can be appreciated by both ancient and modern Australia.

The management of Australian environment has to be accommodated at both a philosophical level and a level of detail suitable for application in management on a day-by-day basis (Hopkins et al. 1990). This invites a synthesis between ancient and modern knowledge, as well as a recognition of spiritual quality in the material world. The challenge is before us and, as this paper demonstrates, it is beginning to be addressed.

REFERENCES

Adamson, D. A., and M. D. Fox. 1982. "Change in Australian Vegetation Since European Settlement," in J. M. B. Smith, ed., *A History of Australian Vegetation*. Pp. 109–146. Sydney: McGraw-Hill.

Andersen, A. N. 1990. "The Use of Ant Communities to Evaluate Change in Australian Terrestrial Ecosystems: A Review and a Recipe." *Proc. Ecol. Soc. Aust.* (New South Wales) 16:347–357.

Bains, G. 1986. "Ecologists and Anthropologists, Unite." *Tradition, Conservation and Development*. Occasional Newsletter of Ecology's Working Group on Traditional Ecological Knowledge, 4, IUCN/Commission on Ecology, Gland.

Beckermann, G. G., and R. J. Coventry. 1987. "Soil Erosion Losses: Squandered Withdrawals from a Diminishing Account." *Search* 18:21–26.

Birch, C. 1990. *On Purpose*. Kensington, NSW: New South Wales University Press.

Blainey, G. 1980. *A Land Half Won*. Melbourne: McMillan.

Bollen, J. D. 1973. Religion in Australian Society: An Historian's View. The Leigh College Open Lectures, Winter Series, New South Wales.

Bowler, J. M. 1976. "Recent Developments in Reconstructing Late Quaternary Environments in Australia," in R. L. Kirk and A. G. Thorne, eds., *Origin of the Australians*. Pp. 55–77. Canberra: Australian Institute of Aboriginal Studies.

Bratton, S. P. 1984. "Christian Ecotheology and the Old Testament." *Environmental Ethics* 6:195–209.

Brown, P. R. 1987. Draft Management Plan for the Conservation of the Eastern Barred Bandicoot *Perameles gunnii* in Victoria. Arthur Rylah Institute of Environmental Research, Heidelberg, Victoria.

Burke, S., and R. Youl. 1990. "The Revegetation of Victoria: The First Stages." *Proc. Ecol. Soc. Aust.* (New South Wales) 16:135–140.

Campbell, B. 1989. "Seven Ages of Conservation Farming in Victoria." *Aust. J. Soil and Water Conserv.* 3(2): 10–13.

Charlesworth, M. 1984. "Introduction," in M. Charlesworth, H. Morphy, D. Bell, and K. Maddock, eds., *Religion in Aboriginal Australia*. Pp. 1–18. St. Lucia: University of Queensland Press.

Clark, I. D. 1990. *Aboriginal Languages and Clans, 1800–1900: An Historical Atlas of Western and Central Victoria*. Monash Publications in Geography No. 37, Monash University, Victoria, Australia.

Clark, R. L. 1983. "Pollen and Charcoal Evidence for the Effects of Aboriginal Burning on the Vegetation of Australia." *Archaeol. Oceania* 28:32–37.

Clark, R. L. 1990. "Ecological History for Environmental Management." *Proc. Ecol. Soc. Aust.* (New South Wales) 16:1–21.

Cobb, J. B., Jr., and D. R. Griffin. 1976. *Process Theology: An Introductory Exposition*. Philadelphia: Westminster Press.

Cochran, A. A. 1972. "Relation Between Quantum Physics and Biology." *Foundations of Physics* 1:235–249.

Coomaraswamy, A. K. 1979. *The Bugbear of Literacy*. Middlesex: Perennial Books.

Coutts, P. J. F., R. K. Frank, and P. Huges. 1978. "Aboriginal Engineers of Western District, Victoria." *Rec. of Vic. Archeol. Survey* 7:1–47.

CSCS (Commonwealth and State Government Collaborative Study). 1978. *A Basis for Soil Conservation Policy in Australia*. Canberra: Australian Govt. Publishing Service.

Davis, S. 1983. Dukarr: The East Arnhem Road Proposal. Report prepared by Landsearch for the Aboriginal Advisory and Development Services, Uniting Church, Northern Synod, Darwin, Australia.

Doing, H. 1981. "Phytogeography of the Australian Floristic Kingdom," in R. H. Groves, ed., *Australian Vegetation*. Pp. 3–25. Sydney: Cambridge University Press.

Downing, J. 1988. Country of My Spirit. Australian National University, Darwin.

Farrer, R. 1908. *In Old Ceylon*. London: Edward Arnold.

Foreman, R. T. T., and M. Godron. 1986. *Landscape Ecology*. New York: John Wiley.

Hobbs, R. J., and A. J. M. Hopkins. 1990. "From Frontier to Fragments: European Impact on Australia's Vegetation." *Proc. Ecol. Soc. Aust.* (New South Wales) 16:93–114.

Hogan, M. 1987. *The Sectarian Strand: Religion in Australian History*. Melbourne: Penguin.

Hooker, J. D. 1860. "On Some of the Naturalized Plants of Australia," in *The Botany (of) the Antarctic Voyage*, Part 3, Flora Tasmaniae, Vol. 1. London: Lovell Reeve.

Hopkins, A. J. M., R. A How, and D. A. Saunders. 1990. "Managing Australia's Environment: Directions for the Future." *Proc. Ecol. Soc. Aust.* (New South Wales) 16:579–583.

Kean, J. S., G. Richardson, and N. Trueman. 1988. Aboriginal Role in Nature Conservation. Emu Conference, Emu, South Australia.

Kershaw, A. P. 1986. "Climate Change and Aboriginal Burning in North-East Australia During the Last Two Glacial/Inter-glacial Cycles." *Nature* 322:47–49.

Kimber, R. G. 1984. "Resource Use and Management in Central Australia." *Aust. Ab. St.* 2:12–23.

Landsat. 1989. Landsat Imagery of the Northern Territory. Department of Conservation, Darwin.

Latz, P. K., and G. F. Griffin. 1978. "Changes in Aboriginal Land Management in Relation to Fire and Food Plants in Central Australia," in B. S.

Hetzel and H. J. Frith, eds., *The Nutrition of Aborigines in Relation to the Ecosystems of Central Australia.* Pp. 78–83. Melbourne: CSIRO.

Leeper, G. W. 1970. "Climate," in G. W. Leeper, ed., *The Australian Environment.* Pp. 12–20. Australia: CSIRO and Melbourne University Press.

Lowenthal, D. 1976. "Perceiving the Australian Environment: A Summary and Commentary," in G. Seddon and M. Davis, eds., *Man and Landscape in Australia: Towards an Ecological Vision.* Pp. 357–365. Canberra: Australian Govt. Publishing Service.

Maddock, K. 1984. "The World Creative Powers," in M. Charlesworth, H. Morphy, D. Bell, and K. Maddock, eds., *Religion in Aboriginal Australia.* Pp. 81–98. St. Lucia: University of Queensland Press.

McDaniel, J. 1986. "Physical Matter as Creative and Sentient." *Environmental Ethics* 5:291

Mcphail, M. K. 1980. "Regeneration Processes in Tasmanian Forests." *Search* 11:184–190.

Naess, A. 1989. *Ecology, Community and Lifestyle: Outline of an Ecophilosophy.* Cambridge: Cambridge University Press.

NSCP (National Soil Conservation Programme). In press. *A Decade of Landcare.* Canberra, Australia.

Oldmeadow, K. 1990. The Religious Tradition of the Australian Aborigines. Occasional Paper of the Sri Lanka Institute of Traditional Studies, Colombo.

Porter, M. 1990. Land of the Spirit? The Australian Religious Experience. World Christian Council Publications, Geneva.

Rackham, O. 1991. "Landscape and the Conservation of Meaning." *Roy. Soc. Arts J.*, pp. 903–915.

Roberts, B. R. 1984. "Land Ethics: A Necessary Addition to Australian Values." Proc. Land Degradation Conference, Australian National University, Canberra.

Rudder, J. 1978. Religion in Aboriginal Studies. Mimeo report. Department of Anthropology, Australian National University, Canberra.

Schuon, F. 1976. *Understanding Islam.* London: Allen & Unwin.

Senanayake, F. R. 1990. "In Defence of Living Soil." *Aust. J. Soil and Water Conserv.* 3(3): 6–7.

Singh, G., A. P. Kershaw, and R. Clark. 1980. "Quaternary Vegetation and Fire History in Australia," in A. M. Gill, R. H. Groves, and I. R. Noble, eds., *Fire and the Australian Biota.* Pp. 23–54. Canberra: Australian Academy of Science.

Stephens, C. G. 1961. *The Soil Landscapes of Australia*. Soil Publication No. 18. Australia: CSIRO.

Strehlow, T. G. H. 1964. Assimilation Problems: The Aboriginal Viewpoint. Aboriginal Advancement League, Inc., of South Australia, Adelaide.

Sullivan K., ed. 1991. *Frogwatch* (Newsletter issued by the Department of Conservation and Environment, Melbourne, Victoria) 1(1): 1–12.

Thorne, A. G. 1981. "The Arrival and Adaptation of Australian Aborigines," in A. Keast, ed., *Ecological Biogeography of Australia*. Pp. 1751–1760. The Hague: Junk.

Tillich, P. 1967. *A History of Christian Thought: From Its Judeo and Hellenistic Origins to Existentialism*. New York: Simon Schuster.

Tindale, N. B. 1974. *Aboriginal Tribes of Australia*. Canberra: Australian National University Press.

Tonkinson, R. 1978. *The Mardudjara Aborigines: Living the Dream in Australia's Desert*. New York: Holt, Rinehart and Winston.

Walker, D., and G. Singh. 1981. "Vegetation History," in R. H. Groves, ed., *Australian Vegetation*. Pp. 26–43. Sydney: Cambridge University Press.

Wallace, P., and N. Wallace. 1977. *Killing Me Softly*. Australia: Thomas Nelson.

Walsh, F. 1990. "Study of Traditional Use of 'Country.'" *Proc. Ecol. Soc. Aust.* (New South Wales) 16:23–37.

Weir, J. S. 1978. The Ant, *Iridomyrmex*, as a Biological Indicator of Pesticide Contamination. New South Wales State Pollution Commission, Sydney.

White, L., Jr. 1967. "The Historical Roots of Our Ecological Crisis." *Science* 155:1203–1207.

Whitehead, A. N. 1978. "Process and Reality," in D. R. Griffin and D. W. Sherbourne, eds., *Process and Reality*. Pp. 45–62. New York: Free Press.

Yeatman, E. M., and P. J. M. Greenslade. 1980. "Ants as Indicators of Habitats in Three Conservation Parks in South Australia." *S. A. Nat.* 55:20–26, 30.

Chapter 6

Managing for Biological Diversity Conservation in Temple Yards and Holy Hills: The Traditional Practices of the Xishuangbanna *Dai* Community, Southwest China

Pei Shengji

Introduction

Global concern for sustainable development and the conservation of biological diversity is dominated by the strategies and styles suitable for today's critically degraded environment. Historically, many societies of indigenous people have formed and established their own traditional conservation methods extending to the protection of plants, animals, and ecosystems based on the ethics, religion, and cultural beliefs of the society.

An indigenous ethnic group in southwest China, the *Dai* (T'ai) people who inhabit Xishuangbanna in the mountainous tropical region, has a long tradition of conservation practices. These practices are characterized by the management of Holy Hills and Buddhist temple yards for conserving biological diversity and habitats, through formal or informal norms and rules of their ethics and religious beliefs. The *Dai's* practices demonstrated the co-existence of biological diversity and cultural diversity and suggested that the principle of biodiversity conservation and the conservation of cultural diversity should be considered as concomitant processes and as integral factors in the conservation of biological diversity today.

THE *DAI* PEOPLE AND THEIR CONSERVATION CULTURE

Xishuangbanna *Dai* autonomous prefecture is one of the eight autonomous prefectures in Yunnan and was established by the People's

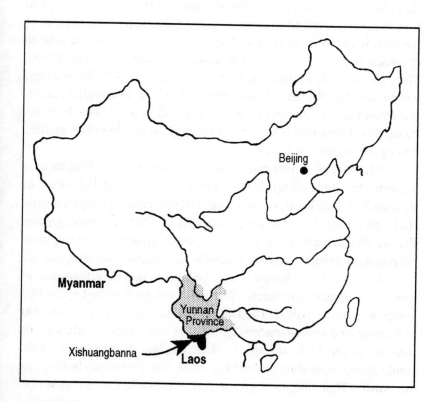

Figure 6.1. Location of the Xishuangbanna *Dai* autonomous prefecture, Yunnan Province, China.

Republic of China in the 1950s to allow for regional autonomy and the preservation of ethnic languages, traditions, customs, and religious beliefs. This prefecture is located in the south of Yunnan Province, in southwest China (24°10'–22°40' N, 99°55'–101°50' E), bordered on the south and southeast by Laos and on the southwest by Myanmar (Figure 6.1). Approximately 94 percent of the total area of 19,220 km² of Xishuangbanna consists of mountainous and hilly terrain; river valleys make up the remaining area. This mountainous zone is a southern extension of the Hengduan Mountains – the eastern append-ages of the Himalayas – where the Upper Lancang Jiang (Mekong) River and its tributaries form the area's major river system. Tropical forests are scattered all over the area and account for 33.8 percent of the total land cover. Some 3,631 species of higher plants have been recorded in the area (Yunnan Institute of Tropical Botany 1983). Thus, one-seventh of the total plant species of China (25,000 species) can be found in Xishuangbanna Prefecture alone, although it consti-tutes only one-five hundredth of the total land area of China. Further-more, this means that it has one of the highest biological diversities among the regions of China.

Much of southwestern China, including Yunnan Province, is inhabited by ethnic groups of non-Han ethnic status and derivation. In Yunnan Province itself, twenty-four different ethnic groups are offi-cially recognized as "national minorities." Overall, these groups display considerable cultural and economic diversity, ranging from hill peoples who practice swidden cultivation and forest management, to lowland dwelling groups whose primary mode of subsistence is intensive wet-rice agriculture. The latter category includes the *Dai* group in Xishuangbanna. The *Dai* people number well over 800,000 in Yunnan and approximately 226,000 of this larger population are concentrated in Xishuangbanna, where the *Dai,* as the largest single ethnic group, constitute about 35 percent. The *Dai* group belongs to the Austro-Thai linguistic group and is classified as a Tai-Kadai subgroup, along with the Zhuang and Bouyei in China (Wang 1988). The *Dai* possess their own dialect and script, both referred to as Daile. The word for Xishuangbanna in Daile is *Sip-song Pan-na*, meaning

"Twelve Administrative Areas."

The *Dai,* as an aboriginal group in the region, were first recorded in Chinese historical texts as far back as the early years of the Han Dynasty (ca. 2000 B.C.), and in these texts the ancestors of the *Dai* people were called *Dain* and *San* (Zheng-Lan 1980). For centuries, the economic situation of the *Dai* was characterized by a local autarky, a self-sufficient economic pattern that combines agriculture with the use of natural products. Although they have long practiced settled agriculture, primarily wet-rice cultivation along with the cultivation of tea, fruits, spices, and herbs, the *Dai* also raise cattle, pigs, and poultry in a semidomesticated manner. In addition, hunting, fishing, and collection of wild plants have played important, traditional roles in the local economy. Consequently, the *Dai* people still depend a great deal on natural plants and animals for their livelihood.

The conservation of nature is essentially part of the *Dai's* traditional culture. The primitive forest philosophy of the *Dai,* and the religious basis of traditional life, bred in the people a respect for life in all its forms and for their own ecological niche. The constant interaction of the *Dai* people with the natural environment would have sharpened their insight into ecoadaptive resource use and conservational strategies. Use of the forests is the most important resource system peculiar to this region. It is believed that forests covered 60 percent of the total area until the 1950s (Pei 1986). There is also no doubt that the agricultural systems in the mountainous region, both the permanent farming system in the valley and the swidden system in the hills, are directly or indirectly supported by mountain forest systems. Furthermore, mountain forests provide various products, environmental protection, and cultural needs for the *Dai* and other smaller groups of mountain people within the region. The *Dai* use different species of plants and animals from their surrounding forests for various purposes. They perceive and manage their environmental resources as their total habitat for their subsistence.

The *Dai* originally followed a polytheistic religion that was heavily bound to the natural world and embraced a forest-oriented philosophy. The *Dai* perception of the interrelationship of human beings with their physical environment is that it consists of five major elements: forest, water, land, food, and humanity. They believe that the forest is a human's cradle. Water comes from the forests, land is fed by the water, and food comes from the land that is fed by the water and the rivers. Human life is supported by the forests, and the forests are one with the supernatural realm (Pei, in press). One of the *Dai* folk songs states "Elephants walk with the forests, the climate with bamboo." Another folk song of Xishuangbanna says "If you cut down all the trees, you have only the bark to eat; if you destroy the forests, you destroy your road to the future" (Wang 1988).

The *Dai* perception is a good example of the cultural value of conservation in which human beings are perceived as a part of the ecosystem, depending on it for survival and development. It is a philosophically refined culture, which in principle rejects the differentiation among species and respects life in all forms extending to plants and animals. This is the philosophy based on the historical ethics and the religion of the *Dai*.

DAI'S TRADITIONAL PRACTICES OF BIOLOGICAL DIVERSITY CONSERVATION

Global concern for sustainable development and the conservation of biological diversity are dominated by the strategies and styles which have critically degraded many environments. Today, the problems of the degraded environment and the loss of biological diversity in many Third World countries are mainly the result of guided development interventions and the overexploitation of natural resources for short-term economic development, rather than development based on the knowledge systems of indigenous communities which have maintained diverse resources for thousands of years. The traditional culture of conservation generated social practices characterized by a number of social norms and rules that regulated human activities to integrate and blend with natural environments. The *Dai's* traditional practices of biological diversity conservation vary from diversification of land use forms; use of a large number of nonwood forest products; cultivation of fuelwood trees; development of homegarden plants and different types of agroforestry; establishment of Holy Hills as community protected areas; and management of diverse plants in temple yards. However, since these overall practices are so diverse, I will only discuss here the two aspects of the Holy Hills and the temple yards, both of which are derived from the traditional cultural beliefs of this ethnic group.

Holy Hills and Conservation of Biodiversity

The worship of plants and animals has been practiced among a number of early societies since ancient times. The *Feng Chan* ritual of China's ancient emperors, which consisted of the worship of a mountain for the protection of mountain forests (Wang 1988); the sacred forests of the Indus; and the hundreds of plants offered in religious worship in Asian countries can be read about in numerous ancient documents and in recent studies (Jain 1987; Chandrakanth et al. 1990; Pei 1984). Thus, it seems to be a widespread fact that religious activities have the function of protecting the surrounding environment and its diversity.

The *Dai* people of Xishuangbanna have practiced a predominantly Buddhist religion since the middle of the Tang dynasty (A.D. 618–907) (Pei 1984). Before the introduction of Hinayana Buddhism, the *Dai* people appear to have practiced a polytheistic religion that was heavily bound to the natural world. Like many early groups, the *Dai* associated the forests, animals, and plants that inhabited them and the forces of nature with the spiritual realm. Proper actions and respect for the gods were believed to result in peace and well-being. Improper activities and disrespect, on the other hand, incurred the wrath of the gods who punished the *Dai* villagers with a variety of misfortunes. Thus, the early *Dai* were encouraged to live in "harmony" with their surroundings.

In the traditional concepts of the *Dai,* the Holy Hill, or *Nong* in their own language, is a forested hill where the gods reside. All the plants and animals that inhabit the Holy Hills are either companions of the gods or sacred living things in the gods' garden. In addition, the

Dai believe that the spirits of great and revered chieftains go to the Holy Hills to live, following their departure from the world of the living (Pei 1984).

Holy Hills are an important visual element on the modern Xishuangbanna landscape and can be found wherever one encounters a hill of virgin forest near a *Dai* village. The Holy Hills are a major component of the traditional *Dai* land management ecosystem, which consists of paddy fields, homegardens, and cultivated fuelwood forests in addition to the naturally forested Holy Hill. In Xishuangbanna, approximately 400 of these hills occupy a total area of roughly 30,000 to 50,000 hectares, or 1.5 to 2.5 percent of the total area of the prefecture (Pei 1984). Unfortunately, however, many of these Holy Hills have been partly disturbed or even totally destroyed in some localities by modern development interventions in the past two decades. Some Holy Hills are now covered with rubber trees or cash crops, particularly in the heavily populated areas within the region.

Traditionally, the Holy Hills constitute a kind of natural conservation area with great biological diversity, founded with the help of the gods, and all animals, land, and sources of water within the area are inviolable. Gathering, hunting, wood-chopping, and cultivation are strictly prohibited activities. Although intimately associated with their beliefs and rituals, the *Dai* people do not keep these hills as cemeteries; areas of burial are confined to separate hills called *Ba hao* in the *Dai* language. The *Dai* people believe that such violations would make the gods angry and that misfortune and disaster will be brought down on them as punishment (Pei 1984). The social mechanism of the *Dai* people in Xishuangbanna has strictly limited human activities on the Holy Hills. The following is an excerpt from the *Dai* text entitled *Admonitions of the Tusi to the Commoners:* "The trees on the Nong mountains 'Holy Hills' cannot be cut. In these forests you cannot cut down trees and construct houses. You cannot build houses on the Nong mountains, you don't want to antagonize the spirits, the gods, or the Buddha" (Anonymous 1958).

There appear to be two types of Holy Hill. The first, *Nong Man* (or *Nong Ban*), refers to a naturally forested hill, usually 10 to 100 hectares, that is worshipped by the inhabitants of a nearby village. Where several adjacent villages form a single, larger community *(Meng)*, another type called *Nong Meng* is frequently found. Forested hills of this second type occupy a much larger area, often hundreds of hectares, and they belong to all the villages in the community. In respecting the Holy Hills, the *Dai* villagers not only keep the sanctity of the Hills, but they also present regular offerings in the hope that the gods will be pleased and protect their health and peace.

Phytogeographically, Xishuangbanna lies in a transitional region between tropical and subtropical zones. Different types of forest vegetation are found in this mountainous region, ranging from rainforest (below 800 meters), seasonal rainforest (between 800 and 900 meters), and evergreen mountain forest (above 900 meters). Almost all Holy Hills are located in the seasonal rainforest areas. This might be explained by the fact that *Dai* villages are settled along the distributive line of seasonal rainforest vegetation in this region. Liu et al. (1990), who conducted a case study from 1988 to 1989, reported that the Species Diversity Index of the Holy Hills was 100 in a 1,500 m^2 area. They further stated that "The constituent of the floristic attributive characters and the species diversity in six Holy Hills was between 75 and 122 in each of the 1,500 m^2 sampling plots." A number of earlier studies conducted by the Yunnan Institute of Tropical Botany, Academia Sinica, indicate that the vegetation on these hills closely resembles the patterns of vegetation in large tracts of pristine, regional forests in terms of character, structure, function, and species composition (Yunnan Institute of Tropical Botany 1983).

Near the village of *Man-yuang-kwang,* located in a tropical, seasonal rainforest area, for example, the Holy Hill has 53 hectares at an altitude of 670 meters above sea level. The Hill's forests contain 311 different plant species belonging to 108 families and 236 genera. The structure of the forest community can be divided into three layers of trees, of which 20 to 30 percent are deciduous or semideciduous in nature: one shrub layer, and one layer each of herbs and seedlings. The forest's ecological characteristics, including energy flow, material flow, and meteorological functions, after 8 years of continuing observation, indicate strong similarities between the patterns of the Holy Hill and those of the tropical, seasonal rainforest nearby.

A case study conducted on the same location of the Holy Hill in 1988 (Liu et al. 1990) showed a significant component change of the forest structure. The study reported that 110 species of plants were recorded in a sampling plot of 1,500 m² in contrast to the record of 75 species in an 1,800 m² sampling plot in the same location in 1958. However, the number of arboreal species of the forest had decreased from 38 in 1958 to 34 in 1988, and the number of the trees had decreased from 177 in 1958 to 93 in 1988 in the same plot. The depleted population belonged to the species of the rainforest elements of the forest vegetation. Simultaneously, changes in other Holy Hills in the region have been observed as well. The main factor causing the deterioration has been the modern development interventions, over the past two decades, that brought about regional changes in land use, which in turn had an impact on the *Dai's* traditional culture. The size of the Holy Hills has been reduced and separated from other kinds of forest, thus creating a generally less tenable situation for the Holy Hills, as well as for the forest species (Liu et al. 1990).

The traditional practice of the Holy Hill concept among the *Dai* people, however, has made a significant contribution to the conservation of biological diversity in the region. First, it has contributed to ecosystem conservation within the ecotone region where there are consequently hundreds of well-preserved dry, seasonal rainforest localities characterized by species of *Antiaris, Pouteria, Canarium,* and others. Second, a large number of endemic, old, or relic species of the local flora have been protected on the Holy Hills. For example, ten species of plants have been identified that are listed in the national priority categories for conservation in the *Red Data Book of Plant for China* (Academia Sinica 1989). In fact, 30 percent of the total species in the Xishuangbanna region fall into this national priority category. Moreover, about 100 species of medicinal plants and more than 150 species of economically useful plants are found on the Holy Hills. Third, the large number of forested Holy Hills distributed throughout the region forms hundreds of "green islands" in the farming fields of the region. This pattern could help the natural reserves, which were established by the State government in recent years, by exchanging genes and playing the role of "stepping stones" for the flow of biological gene materials between the natural reserves and the Holy Hills. The natural reserves are separated into five large sections and seven locations totaling 334,576 hectares and ideally surrounded by larger and smaller Holy Hills (Liu et al. 1990).

Managing for Biodiversity Conservation in Temple Yards

The Hinayana Buddhism of the *Dai* has been infused with ethnic color and is still popular among the *Dai* villagers. Today, Buddhist temples, or *Wa* in the *Dai* language, are found in most villages. Historical records suggest that there were once more than 360 temples in the area; and of these, about 220 still exist (Pei 1984).

Buddhist culture requires its followers to recognize that one should not differentiate between human and nonhuman species with respect to suffering (Gupta and Ura 1990). Furthermore, the canons of Buddhism specify that four requirements must be met before a Buddhist temple can be established. These requirements are (1) a statue of Sakyamuni *(Pagodama-Zhao in Dai)*, the founder of Buddhism; (2) a pagoda in which Sakyamuni's ashes can be preserved; (3) five monks, at least; and (4) the presence of specified "temple yard plants" (Pei 1984; Gogoi et al. 1990). According to the classic "Records of the Buddhas" (coming into the world for 28 generations), of which there is a handwritten copy in *Dai*, the Buddha of each generation designated one species of plant as the adored plant for Buddhists. All of these adored plants have been identified recently as tree species native to South Asian or Southeast Asian regions, including Xishuangbanna. These trees are considered *"Nong* trees" or sacred trees by the *Dai* people. They are cultivated in the temple yards with other trees, shrubs, and herbaceous plants as offerings for Buddha. *"Nong* trees" are also planted in the villages, on roadsides, or near drinking water sources in the *Dai* area. It is strictly forbiden to harm *Nong* trees. According to the customary law of the *Dai*, cutting down any of these trees is taboo. In the *Admonitions of the Tusi to the Commoners* (Anonymous 1958), it is recorded that "You cannot fell *Nong* trees in the villages or any other place; you ought to protect trees near the village. You must not cut them down." In the regulations for fines and penalties, it further says, "If you cut down the sacred trees of another village, you must pay a sacrificial fee; otherwise people may die in that village, and, if they do, then you must pay 1,500 dollars per person" (Wang 1988).

The temple yards of the Buddhist temples normally contain dozens of species of tropical plants that are cultivated in line with the creed of the Buddhist canons. An earlier investigation (Pei 1984) on plants in temple yards reported that more than fifty-eight different species of commonly cultivated plants have been recorded from twenty-two temple yards in the region. These species can be grouped into three types according to the Buddhist culture.

- Group I. Ritual plants: Total of twenty-one species, including all *Nong* trees such as *Aegle marmelos, Borassus flabellifer, Corypha umbraculifera, Dipterocarpus turbinatus, Ficus altissima, F. glomerata, F. religiosa, Gmelina arborea, Livestona saribus, Mayodendron igneum, Mesua nagassarium, Millingtonia hortensis, Parkia leiophylla, Streblus asper, Tectona grandis.*

- Group II. Fruit trees: Total of seventeen species, such as *Anona reticulata, A. squamosa, Artocarpus heterophylla, Citrus grandis, Cocos nucifera, Flacoutia romontchii, Litchi chinensis, Syzygium jambos, Tamarindus indica,* including many of the tropical fruits. The fruits are normally used as offerings at Buddhist ceremonies and are also served as daily food for monks at the temple.

- Group III. Ornamental plants: Total of twenty species, including *Butea monosperma, Cassia fistula, Crinum asiaticum, Delonix regia, Gardenia jasminoides, G. sootepense, Gendarusa*

venticosa, Michelia alba, M. champac, Nymphaea spp.,
Plumeria acutifolia, Samanea saman, Sesbanea grandiflora.
These plants play a role in beautifying the temple, and the
flowers of these plants can be used for offerings in Buddhist
worship.

Historically, managing temple yard plants in Xishuangbanna is
not only limited to religious purposes but, more significantly in terms
of maintaining biological diversity, it serves as a means of introducing
and domesticating plants from outside the region as well as the wild
species of local flora. Accordingly, among the fifty-eight temple yard
plants, more than twenty-nine species are from India or tropical South
Asia; nineteen species are from China or Southeast Asia; and ten
species are from either tropical America or Africa. The presence of
nonendemic plant species in the temple yards (later distributed over
the region and to other parts of Yunnan) is historically related to the
spread and acceptance of Hinayana Buddhism among the *Dai* within
the last 1,400 years. However, some plant species of local flora
cultivated in the temple yards were primarily cultivated in the temple
yards for religious use or because of the values of Buddhist ethics. In
this sense, the Buddhist temple yards of the region have played an
important role in the *ex situ* conservation of plant species. Similar to
the role of botanical gardens in Western culture, they could be called
"Temple-Botanical Gardens." The well-known Man-Jinlan Public
Park at Jing Hong City in Xishuangbanna is part of the temple yard of
the Man-Jinlan Village.

Although the *Dai* of Xishuangbanna do not prohibit the hunting
of birds, if a bird enters the village, the people generally do not permit
it to be shot. Several *Dai* documents contain regulations that prohibit
the shooting of birds near houses. For instance, a sentence in *Regulations Concerning Fines and Penalties* states: "It is prohibited to use
a gun to shoot a bird while it is sitting on another man's granary. The
fine is 3 dollars." The *Dai* are strictly prohibited from hunting any
wildlife that is white. They believe that all such wildlife, particularly
large, white wild animals, are sacred. This taboo might be because

white wild animals are unusual among the local fauna. This has certainly helped in the protection of rare wildlife species.

CONCLUSION: THE CO-EXISTENCE OF BIOLOGICAL DIVERSITY AND CULTURAL DIVERSITY

The relationship between natural resources and the people has been forged within moral, cultural, political-economic, and ecological boundaries. Respect for these boundaries by different communities and social groups was the result of historically accepted formal and informal rules and norms (Gupta and Ura 1990). The forest-oriented philosophy and the religious basis of traditional life have bred in the *Dai* people of Xishuangbanna a respect for forests, plants, animals, and their own ecological niche, through these formal and informal norms and rules of their society. The conservation culture of the *Dai*, combined with indigenous management strategies for natural resources for productive purposes, succeeded in maintaining the forests of this region at a high percentage of coverage and in managing biological diversity in their environment very effectively over a long time. These factors can be seen as an example of the positive impact of the interaction of human culture with the environment and the conservation of biological diversity that existed in many earlier societies.

Human culture is built upon and developed on the basis of the physical world, and they are interdependent on each other. Cultural diversity, hence, largely depends on the biological diversity which provides tangible materials in enormous varieties for humans from which to establish societies and lifestyles. As the Xishuangbanna region is characterized by a wide biological diversity and ethnic cultural traditions, the *Dai* people have developed their own traditional culture which is based on the available resources in their surrounding environment. These include food, medicine, decoration, religion, ritual, recreation, protection, arts, literature, music, and folkloric traditions. All of these depend on biological resources and natural systems. On the other hand, although the cultural diversity of ethnic groups in the region has modified the component and distributive patterns of biological resources through human practices in the process of production and cultural beliefs, this has not had a negative impact on the biological diversity in the environment. The presence of the *Dai's* Holy Hills and temple yards is a good example of these synergistic relationships.

Other approaches for conserving the biological diversity of the *Dai* people, which have not been discussed, are the conservation practices of biological species while they are being used. *Dai* people have protected biological species in their surroundings as much as possible through sustainable use of biological resources and ecosystems. They have also increased the degree of biodiversity in their habitats through the selection, domestication, cultivation, and breeding of useful plants and animals, which has resulted in a broader gene pool. Along with providing material needs such as food, medicine, and shelter, plants have been closely associated with many of the social customs and religious rituals of humans (Jain 1987). Many flowers, fruits, or whole plants have been protected for use in offerings in worship, and some plants are themselves worshipped or considered sacred.

The principle of the co-existence of biological diversity and cultural diversity has resulted in distinctive physical phenomena in the landscape of the *Dai* people in Xishuangbanna. The Holy Hills with natural forest vegetation, the temple yard plants with many native and introduced species, the sacred trees in or nearby the *Dai* villages, and a number of religious plants and traditional social activities all have become a part of the *Dai* life. The interdependence of cultural diversity and biological diversity has strongly demonstrated that the principle of co-existence of both diversities has been established through the process of human history. Thus, it suggests that the conservation of biodiversity and cultural diversity should be considered as integral needs in the process of development today.

REFERENCES

Academia Sinica, Institute of Botany. 1989. Vol. 1, *The Red Data Book of Plants for China.* Beijing, China: Science Publishing Press.

Anonymous. 1958. A Series of Chinese Translations of *Dai* Documents. Kunming, China.

Chandrakanth, M. G., J. K. Gilless, V. Gowramma, and M. G. Nagaraja. 1990. Temple Forests in India's Forest Department. Working Paper. University of California, Berkeley.

Gogoi, P., and S. K. Borthakur. 1990. Plants Used in Religiocultural Beliefs of the Tai Khamatis (of India). Paper presented at the 2nd International Congress of Ethnobiology, 22–26 October, Kunming, China.

Gupta, A. K., and K. Ura. 1990. Blending Cultural Values, Indigenous Technology and Environment: Experiences in Bhutan. Paper presented at the International Symposium on Strategies for Sustainable Mountain Development, 10–14 September, ICIMOD, Kathmandu, Nepal.

Jain, S. K. 1984. *A Manual of Ethnobotany.* Jodhpur, India: Scientific Publishers.

Liu, Hongmo, Xu Zhaifu, and Fao Guoda. 1990. *Dai* Holy Hills of Xishuangbanna and the Conservation of Plant Diversity in Tropical Rain Forests. Paper presented at the 2nd International Congress of Ethnobiology, 22–26 October, Kunming, China.

Pei, Shengji. 1985. "Some Effects of the *Dai* People's Cultural Beliefs and Practices on the Plant Environment of Xishuangbanna, Yunnan Province, Southwest China," in K. L. Hutterer, A. T. Rambo, and G. Lovelace, eds., *Cultural Values and Human Ecology in Southeast Asia.* Pp. 321–339. Paper No. 27. Ann Arbor: University of Michigan.

Pei, Shengji. 1986. Tropical Forests and Upper Watershed Management. Paper presented at the Workshop on Ecological Principles for Watershed Management, 7–11 April, East–West Center, Honolulu, HI.

Pei, Shengji. In press. "The Contribution of Ethnobiology to Agricultural Development." *Entwickland and Landicher Raum* (Germany).

Wang, Ningsheng. 1988. Preservation and Development of Minority Cultures in S. W. China: A Case Study on Ethnobiology. Paper presented at the 12th International Congress of Anthropological and Ethnological Sciences, 24–31 July, Zagreb, Yugoslavia.

Yunnan Institute of Tropical Botany, Chinese Academy of Sciences. 1983. *Plant List of Xishuangbanna.* China: Yunnan Ethnic Publishing House.

Zheng-Lan. 1980. *Travels Through Xishuangbanna: China's Sub-Tropical Home of Many Nationalities.* Beijing: Foreign Language Press.

Chapter 7

Traditional Resource Management and the Conservation of Biological Diversity on Pohnpei Island, Federated States of Micronesia

Herson Anson and William Raynor

Introduction

There was a man *Sapkini* who made a canoe that was large and deep, that would be sufficient for many people to ride in. He then called together the crew of the vessel. ... They started out and sailed forth. ...

Now there was an exposed part of a reef, on which there was a little piece of coral. It had no vegetation on it ... and they gave the piece of coral the name *Tierensapw* (a bit of land). They inspected and supposedly it would be good for becoming land. Now the day when they reached that place, the canoe spanned the bit of coral. ...

They started their work of making land. They built up the land and spread it out so that it might make a level place. Their work kept getting larger and larger ... (but) the land could not be really good for the waves of the sea kept splashing it apart. They then called on *Katinanik* to come and protect the land from waves. However this was not successful as the open sea was too close to the edge of the land. ... They then called *Katenenior* to come and surround the land. Now *Katenenior* was the barrier reef and *Katinanik* is the mangrove. ...

Now the project was satisfactory and the land became better, and all things were settled. When the platform became large and formed a land they gave it the name of *Pei* (stone structure) and everything that was on top of this rock they called *Pohnpei* (Upon the stone altar) ... (from Barnhart 1977).

Pohnpei beliefs and culture (*tiahk en Pohnpei*) have always influenced humanity's relationship with nature. The foundation of the Pohnpei culture rests on the belief that Pohnpei was built by the original settlers, and all plants and animals were brought to the island by civilization. However, this belief, rather than justifying a wide-scale exploitation and destruction of resources, has instead led to an attitude of stewardship. This culturally based respect for the natural environment, along with a favorable climate and rough topography, is obvious even today in the relative abundance of biologically diverse upland and mangrove forest compared with other Micronesian islands. However, one result of the rapid development characterizing Pohnpei today is a weakening of the cultural beliefs that have governed Pohnpeians' relationships with the natural environment. Population pressure, road and house construction, timber extraction, and farming are only a few of the pressures facing Pohnpei's native forests and wetlands. This paper seeks to document some of the traditional cultural beliefs that have led to the maintenance of biological diversity in the past, and examine what, if any, relevance these beliefs have in modern Pohnpei.

POHNPEI ISLAND

The island of Pohnpei is located in the Caroline islands of the western Pacific (Figure 7.1). It is the highest and second largest island in the chain and is the capital of the Federated States of Micronesia. Rainfall is high (191 inches/year) and well-distributed throughout the year, and temperatures average a year-round 82° F.

Typical of the humid climate, vegetation on Pohnpei is characterized by several types of forest, with only small areas of open savannah. Nearly 94 percent of the island was covered by forest in

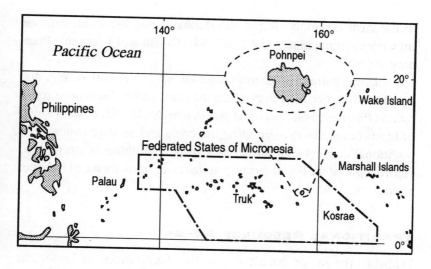

Figure 7.1. Pohnpei Island, Federated States of Micronesia.
Source: MacLean et al. 1986.

1983 (MacLean et al. 1986). Upland areas are characterized by *Campnosperma breviopetiolata* – dominant upland forest, and *Clinostigma ponapensis* – dominant palm forest, with small amounts of swamp and cloud forest. At middle and lower elevations, pockets of upland forest are mixed with secondary vegetation and agroforest. Toward the coast, secondary vegetation and agroforest become dominant. The entire island is ringed by an extensive mangrove forest, in some areas nearly 2 miles thick.

The majority of the people live in the rural areas, scattered over individual farmsteads. Although many live near the coast, inland habitation has accelerated greatly with increasing population pressure. Subsistence agriculture and fishing are still the main occupation of many inhabitants, though wage jobs in government and a fledgling private industry have lured many to participate, at least peripherally, in the cash economy. Rapid development has led to an extreme import:export imbalance (32:1 in 1984) (Division of Economic Planning 1986).

Local cultural tradition (*tiahk en sahpw*) is still strong, and people must work hard to produce the giant yams (*Dioscorea* spp.), *sakau* (*Piper methysticum*), and pigs demanded by the constant round of feasts (*kamadipw*) celebrating life crisis and prestige events. The traditional concept of a farmer as a surplus producer is strong, and *sapwasapw*, or the life of farming, remains a central theme of Pohnpei culture.

TRADITIONAL RESOURCE AREAS

Probably the major contributor to the maintenance of biological diversity on Pohnpei has been the recognition of different resource areas. Pohnpeians traditionally recognize several such areas, and each is governed by certain aspects that define the human role and interaction with the natural components of the area. At the broadest level, there is the *nansed*, or the sea, and *nansapw*, the land. For purposes of this paper, we will concentrate on *nansapw*.

Nansapw is divided into two major contrasting classifications, *nanwel* and *nansapw*, by Pohnpeians. The third area recognized, which is neither land nor sea, is *naniahk*, or the mangrove forest. The term *nanwel* (or *nanwoal* in the dialect of Kitti municipality) refers to (1) the mountainous areas that are typically covered with dense wild forest, and (2) land that has been abandoned long enough to have reverted to quasi-wild forest. On the other hand, *nansapw* refers to (1) the flat areas and narrow plains between the mountainous areas, and (2) the cleared, utilized, and/or cultivated lands. *Nansapw*, then, refers mainly to "humanized" lands where humans settle, reside, and cultivate crops, in comparison with *nanwel*, the "wild" lands or lands outside human authority. This dichotomy is inherent in the Pohnpei mentality and is a major determinant in the maintenance of biological diversity, especially in the *nanwel* areas.

The Upland Forest (Nanwel)

The *nanwel*, and to a lesser extent the *naniahk*, was and still is recognized as lived in and ruled by *eni*, literally spirits or gods. Although traditional Pohnpei religion has been mostly replaced by Christianity today, nevertheless the belief in *eni* residing in the *nanwel* is vividly retained and still is used to explain and interpret many daily events, both social and natural, which "are wholly unexpected, quite unlucky, seriously disastrous or extremely mysterious" (Shimizu 1982). A few of the *eni* still believed to inhabit the *nanwel* are *Lipopohnwoal*, the *eni* culture hero *Nahnisopahu*, and the trickster puppet-like *eni Sokolai*.

The Pohnpei attitude toward the *nanwel* is ambivalent. On one hand, the *nanwel* is the very basis on which Pohnpeians credit nature with the power of sustaining human existence on the island. Conversely, the *nanwel* is the *eni's* land, where the customary rules regarding human affairs largely cease to work. One example is that while in the upland forest, people can no longer call to each other by name, for fear that an *eni* may identify and allure that person. Instead, people call and answer each other by shouting "uh, uh," similar to a wild animal's cry. Another example is that trips in the upland forest are generally short – limited to 1 or 2 days. The concept of living in the upland forest is beyond consideration to most Pohnpeians, due to the risk of various supernatural dangers one might encounter with prolonged contact with the various *eni* there. New homesteads in the upland forest always go through a transitional process known as *sapwasapw* – literally transforming the area to *nansapw* – and newly cleared lands are known as *sahpwkapw* (new lands). The primary relations in the jungle then are not of people to people, but rather people to *eni*.

From a utilization perspective, the *nanwel* is also considered outside of the daily human social and cultural boundaries. Upland forest plants and animals may be eaten, but cannot be used in presentations or other cultural exchange rituals.

The Mangrove (Naniahk)

The *naniahk* is also believed to be inhabited and ruled by *eni*. Again, many of the unexplained events, especially illness, are blamed on the *eni* in the *naniahk; soumwahu en naniahk* (literally mangrove sickness) is one of the most common illnesses among Pohnpeians according to local medicine practitioners. Other beliefs also exist. In Enipein, a village in Kitti municipality, a stand of mangrove is never disturbed. It is believed that if a tree in this stand is cut or even falls naturally, an individual of the major clan in Kitti will die. No doubt these beliefs have been important in the preservation of the mangrove forest on Pohnpei.

TRADITIONAL PLANT USES

Another major factor in the maintenance of plant biodiversity on Pohnpei has been the importance of plants to the Pohnpeians' life. For centuries, plants have been used in ceremonies, for food, shelter, transportation, as cures for diseases and pains, and other everyday needs.

Ceremonial Uses

An important part of being a Pohnpeian is participation in the traditional culture, which includes numerous events and other ceremonies. This type of work is *doadoahk en wahu* (work of respect), since Pohnpei culture revolves around respect. *Doadoahk en wahu* is divided into *tou*, a contribution to the chiefs that is voluntarily performed, and *pwukoah*, those contributions assigned to subjects as their obligation to the chiefs. The obligatory contributions are composed of *nohpwei* and *kamadipw*. *Nohpwei* is generally translated as the tribute of the "first fruit," whereas *kamadipw* is the practice of large-scale feast ceremonies.

Nohpwei. The *nohpwei* is the obligatory tribute of *mwowe* (the first one) of certain crops to the chiefs. The meaning of the term *mwowe* varies from plant to plant, and thus results in many different types of *nohpwei* tributes (Shimizu 1982):

Seasonal *nohpwei*:	*mahi* (breadfruit)
	kehp (yam)
	kipar (pandanus)
Instrumental *nohpwei*:	*sakau* (*Piper methysticum*)
	sehu (sugarcane)
	uht (banana)
	mwahng (*Cyrtosperma* taro)
Occasional *nohpwei*:	*sakau*

The seasonal *nohpwei* is highly formalized and is still practiced widely, especially for breadfruit and yam. The *nohpwei* for breadfruit and yams is defined by the various stages of growth. Seasonal *nohpwei* tributes are performed by each *kousapw* (subsection of the municipality) as a presentation to the paramount chiefs. Later, members of each *kousapw* may also perform the *nohpwei* tribute to their own *kousapw* chief, the *soumas*.

Instrumental *nohpwei* differs from the seasonal *nohpwei* in that the *mwowe* of these plants is defined in terms of the fields in which they are cultivated. When someone clears land, or enlarges an existing planting and then successfully harvests the crop, that person brings the first crop to the chiefs. This type of *nohpwei* is only rarely practiced today.

Only *sakau* (*Piper methysticum*) can be used in the last type, the occasional *nohpwei*. Since *sakau* transcends all other crops in its *wahu* value, it is the key component in nearly all traditional activities. *Sakau* is presented and prepared during meetings, when asking for favors or asking forgiveness for particularly serious transgressions, for marriage ceremonies, and various other occasions when a commoner needs to meet with higher titled Pohnpeians or paramount chiefs.

Kamadipw. *Kamadipws*, or feasts, are generally held to recognize crucial events in people's lives (e.g., the peak of the yam harvest, the coronation of chiefs, acceptance of titles, deaths). *Kamadipws* are performed with a single intricate ritual, regardless of the event or size of gathering. Paramount chiefs or high-titled family members at smaller family feasts preside over the *kamadipw* as honored guests. The tribute of the five important prestige items – yams, breadfruit, *sakau*, pigs, or dogs – is obligatory for all mature male participants, and the sheer size and amount of these items are aptly described by the English translation of the word *kamadipw*, which literally means "to beat the bush."

An important concept in Pohnpei culture is the distinction between crops that can be used for *doadoahk en wahu*, and those restricted from such use. In general, animals and plants that are regarded to be wild (regenerate spontaneously and grow with little or no care from humans) and those that are recently introduced are considered unsuitable for *doadoahk en wahu*. On the other hand, these foodstuffs are common in the everyday diet of most people. For plants, this distinction can be further broken down into annuals and perennials. Perennial plants (i.e., trees) tend to be seasonal to semiseasonal on Pohnpei. Generally the main fruiting season for all tree crops is from late March to August, the season known as the *rahk* (time of plenty). Plants that bear during this season are generally felt to be more influenced by nature than by direct human actions, although a bad *rahk* (especially of breadfruit) is often blamed on human divergence from the accepted ways of culture. In contrast, plants that fruit or mature during September to March, the season known as the *isol* (time of little), are generally associated with human labor. Foremost among these are the yam, which is the premier prestige crop on Pohnpei. Yam-growing skills are considered one of the most desirable and to-be-envied qualities of a real Pohnpeian.

Timber. The traditional Pohnpeian's choice of timber species has been mainly limited to requirements for shelter, transportation, and, to a lesser extent, other needs for timber in gardening (e.g., fences, trellises). Pohnpeians use any number of species to satisfy single needs or one species to satisfy several needs; that is, many of the important timber species are somewhat interchangeable in their uses. For example, the breadfruit can be adzed to produce planks for flooring or can be used for constructing a traditional canoe (*wahr*). Pohnpeians living close to the coast use various mangrove species for construction of shelters and use the nipa palm (*Nipa fruiticans*) for thatching. Upland dwellers, on the other hand, use *katar* (*Cyathea* spp.) and *ais* (*Parinari laurina*) for house construction and the endemic ivory nut palm (*Metroxylon amicarum*) for roof thatch.

Some of the common species used for timber are listed:

sohm (*Bruguiera gymnorhiza*)	*ahk* (*Rhizophora* spp.)
mahi (*Artocarpus* sp.)	*ais* (*Parinari laurina*)
keleu (*Hibiscus tiliaceus*)	*katar* (*Cyathea nigricans*)
weipwul (*Morinda citrifolia*)	*nih* (*Cocos nucifera*)
dohng (*Campnosperma brevipetiolata*)	

Many of the common species used for timber also have uses in other categories (i.e., medicine, ceremony). Thus an important concept with many Pohnpei plants is that most are "multipurpose." For example, although *weipwul* (*Morinda citrifolia*) is sometimes used for shelter construction, it is also commonly used in curing a number of ailments. Another species that is valuable in its timber uses, as well as its medicinal value, is *katar* (*Cyathea* sp.) It is the choice species for support of house structures even for shoreline dwellers, provided that it is available within a reasonable distance for collection. It is resistant to weather, as well as insect damage, and can last for more than 20 years. It is also one of the very few known cures for bleeding and is used to lessen the effect of menstruation for women. It also has a "suturing" effect on wounds because, it is believed, of its sticky red sap.

For the Pohnpeian's transportation needs, any one of the varieties of breadfruit (*Artocarpus* sp.) can be used for canoe construction. Other popular hardwoods for canoes include *sadak*

(*Elaeocarpus carolinensis*) and *dohng* (*Campnosperma brevipetiolata*). Species used for constructing the outrigger, though, are not interchangeable. For example, the outrigger and larger poles that hold the dugout and the outrigger together are almost always made of *keleu* (*Hibiscus tiliaceus*), and the smaller poles are always made of *ketieu* (*Ixora* sp.).

Magic and Medicine

Medicinal needs have no doubt contributed considerably to the conservation of biological diversity of plant species on Pohnpei. Some Pohnpeians claim that nearly all plants on Pohnpei have some medicinal or magical use. The situation grows more complicated when it is realized that some single plant species can be used to cure several ailments, while, conversely, a single sickness or disease can be cured by several plant species. For example, the *weipwul* (*Morinda citrifolia*) is used for curing a number of ailments, the bark used for treating some ailments, while the crushed fruit is used for others.

Some commonly known medicinal plants used on Pohnpei include:

weipwul (*Morinda citrifolia*)   *ikoik* (*Cordia subcordata*)

wihnmar (*Barringtonia asiatica*)   *ilau* (*Clerodendrum inerme*)

topwuk (*Premna obtusifolia*)   *ongalap* (*Curcuma* sp.)

Recorded knowledge regarding medicinal uses of plants on Pohnpei is relatively scarce, due to the great secretiveness associated with local medicine on the island. No medicine person (*sounwini*) or magician (*sounwinani*) would freely reveal to others the plants used in creating medicines or magic spells for cure or curse. This knowledge is communicated only to a son or other close relative by choice or upon death. Although this secretiveness is partly because of the compensation that medicine preparers receive from the family of a sick person, it probably is more from the persistent belief on Pohnpei that revealing a medicine causes it to lose its potency. Knowledge of plants used in medicines can either be passed down from close, older relatives or they can be given in a dream, often by a deceased relative who appears before the sleeping medicine person and details the plants to use and how to prepare them. In a village where one of the authors resides, a lady was given instructions in her dream by a deceased family member to collect a certain plant and use it for her husband who was suffering from diabetes and high blood pressure. Not only was the husband cured from his ailment, but this lady has gone on to cure several other patients who had been informed by hospital doctors that their ailments were so advanced that cure was impossible. Medicine persons often specialize in certain types of diseases, and many become well-known for their cures. For medicine and magic, plants are either applied alone or with other items such as oil and pebbles. They are often applied while medicine persons chant or whisper words.

Medicines fall into many categories. A common type of medicine today is one used to return the soul or spirit of a patient, especially children. It is believed when children are surprised (*pwuriamwei*), their spirits may depart from them, causing them to become critically ill. Special spirit doctors, who use certain medicinal plants, can return the soul or spirit. In some cases the patient is beyond cure; the spirit doctor is unable to find the particular part of a plant for the cure even if the plant is located, because the spirit will have already removed the "part" before the doctor gets the plant. Some medicinal plants are also used to cure ailments such as when a ghost of an ancestor enters someone's body and causes illness, because the ancestor is upset at that person or family.

Other Traditional Uses

Fishing. To Pohnpeians, like most islanders, fish is an important source of protein in the diet; therefore, a number of plants had been used for various fishing activities long before the introduction of metal hooks, fiberglass boats, and the casting rod. Other than the plants used for canoes (see Timber), plants were used for fish poison (e.g., *Derris* sp.) and for spears and nets. For spears, *ketieu* (*Ixora* sp.) and *kedei* (*Ptychosperma ledermaniana*) were mainly used. Fibrous plants such as the *keleu* (*Hibiscus tiliaceus*) and coconut (*Cocos nucifera*) were used for making strands for fishing nets.

Clothing. Before cloth was introduced commercially, Pohnpei men used the fibers of *keleu* (*Hibiscus tiliaceus*) for their traditional *koal* (grass skirt). Women wore a wraparound made of pounded breadfruit bark. *Pandanus* fibers were also woven and used for making clothing.

Weapons. The most popular weapon used by the traditional Pohnpeian warriors was the spear, commonly made from *ketieu* (*Ixora* sp.) and *kedei* (*P. ledermaniana*). It was only after the machete was introduced that the local weapons lost their uses.

Containers and Baskets. Traditionally, the coconut frond was more commonly used for making baskets than *Pandanus* species on Pohnpei, though the latter was used occasionally. The coconut basket was generally used as a pantry, where left-over food was kept for visitors.

DIMINISHING TRADITIONAL USES OF PLANTS

Traditional reliance on plants in Pohnpei, as in most of the Pacific islands, is decreasing. Although this decrease is not occurring at an alarming rate, nevertheless, if not held in check, much valuable knowledge may disappear altogether. On Pohnpei, cash is beginning to replace *sakau*, yams, pigs, and dogs in the obligatory *kamadipw en wou*. Also, local foods – especially breadfruit, banana, taro, and yam, upon which most traditions are based – are losing their appeal against the omnipresent imported rice both at home and in cultural events. Imported rice or rice and canned meat are even being served at *kamadipws* as *ahmwadang*, in place of local food, before the *uhmw* is opened and its contents distributed.

The medicinal values of local medicinal plants are not faring any better. Despite a persistent belief that local plant medicines have more potent healing power, they are now often used only as a last resort. It was more convenient in 1990 to visit a medical doctor at the going price of $3 for most complaints.

The convenience of Western technology is also contributing to less dependence on local resources. The refrigerator has not only replaced the intricately woven basket for storing food, but the knowledge of weaving is being lost simultaneously. And for those who cannot afford the price of an electric range, a kerosene stove is more convenient than cooking with the abundantly available firewood, even in remote villages.

Not all Western technology has had a negative influence on the dependence of local resources. For example, the use of outboards helps tremendously in fishing activities by supplementing locally derived protein requirements in addition to imported meat. However, the knowledge of building local canoes is disappearing rapidly and, ironically, the only means of reviving this knowledge may be through grants from overseas (e.g., the U.S. Job Training Partnership Act program).

POSSIBILITIES AND STRATEGIES FOR REVIVING LOCAL RESOURCE USES

Perhaps the most effective strategy in reviving traditional Pohnpeian beliefs to ensure future maintenance of biological diversity against rapid modernization is to digress backward toward the past at a rate faster than that of modernization. But Pohnpeians strongly believe that the only creature that travels backward faster than forward is the *likedepw*, a shrimp-like creature, whose head, although larger than its body, contains few brains. They say, "A Pohnpeian who desires to follow the *likedepw* is no different from one."

The strategies for reviving traditional beliefs in the use of local resources, then, have to be planned and presented to the people in such a way that they will accept them along with the Western lifestyle. There is still hope and time to do this because most people still relate strongly to the land, more so than is immediately obvious. For instance, when the Pohnpei Upland Forest Watershed Preserve (established on paper in 1987 by the Pohnpei State Legislature) was proposed to the people in the communities, the reaction was extremely negative since the watershed provisions were likely to limit their traditional rights to freedom of access into the upland forest.

It is hoped that with increasing awareness for the necessity of watersheds, parks, and biological and historic preserves, the traditional beliefs in the value of our local resources will be safeguarded and enhanced.

REFERENCES

Barnhart, L. 1977. *The Book of Luelen*. Translated and edited by J. Fischer, S. Riesenberg, and M. Whiting. Honolulu, HI: University Press of Hawai'i.

Division of Economic Planning. 1986. Economic and Social Statistics of Pohnpei. Pohnpei State Government, Kolonia, Pohnpei, FSM.

MacLean, C., T. Cole, C. Whitesell, M. Falanruw, and A. Ambacher. 1986. *Vegetation Survey of Pohnpei, Federated States of Micronesia*. USDAPSW Source Bulletin PSW-18, Berkeley, CA.

Shimizu, A. 1982. "Chiefdom and the Spatial Classification of the Life-World: Everyday Life, Subsistence and the Political System on Pohnpei," in M. Aoyagi, ed., *Islanders and Their Outside World: A Report of the Cultural Anthropological Research in the Caroline Islands of Micronesia in 1980–81*. Pp. 153–215. Committee for Micronesian Research, St. Paul's (Rikkyo) University, Tokyo.

Chapter 8

CHRISTIAN DENOMINATIONAL INFLUENCES ON ATTITUDES TOWARD RESOURCES DEVELOPMENT: MAROVO LAGOON, SOLOMON ISLANDS

Sonia P. Juvik

INTRODUCTION

If the grand epic of human life is to be sustained, the widespread and accelerating environmental degradation at every corner of the earth must be fettered. This imperative embodies the following challenges: maintenance of biological diversity, reduction of environmental pollution, and elimination of poverty and powerlessness. The imperative, in essence, calls for the promotion of a meaning system capable of producing ecologically sustainable human-environmental relations *and* "authentic" relations among human beings (see Goulet, 1990, for an excellent discussion of "authentic development"). But it would be instructive to first explore the question of whether or not any of the existing ethics, such as "the land ethic" advanced by Aldo Leopold (1949) or the various religious ethics, contain potentialities for ecologically sustainable outcomes.

In this paper I make the general assertion that religion, or an intellectual tradition largely informed by religious philosophy, is certainly an important, if not primary, force capable of shaping social relations and environmental relations. It is recognized, however, that the explicit role of religion in shaping environmental attitudes and decisions over the use of resources diminishes as societies shift from traditional to market-oriented economies. The specific question I pose here is: Are there religious philosophies which are more ecologically sustaining than others? My question in no way presupposes that any religion is incapable of reducing biological diversity. Rather, I seek to point to those religious beliefs and practices that appear to offer more or less hope for promoting healthful human survival on the planet. To offer some preliminary answers I will present data from Solomon Islands where, in 1987, I undertook an "environmental attitude and awareness survey" among villagers in the Marovo Lagoon Region of the Western Province (see location maps, Figures 8.1 and 8.2). The purpose of that research was to ascertain Marovan's understanding of basic ecological processes and to record their attitudes toward the development of their natural resources.

It is possible to identify at least three dominant viewpoints concerning the relationship between humans and nature that imply differences which can affect the preservation of biological diversity and overall attitudes toward the natural world. The first view is one in which nature and the creator are one and is characteristic of animistic religions predominating in tribal societies. Fear and respect for the sacredness of natural objects, as well as the imposition of strong sanctions against wastefulness, are hallmarks of human-environmental relations in animistic societies. (For further discussion of traditional environmental attitudes, see Martin 1978, Malo 1951, Valeri 1985, and Dudley in this volume.) In the second view, human beings and nature are on an equal footing and human beings are stewards of the land and must seek to understand and harmonize with natural processes. This belief system permeates eastern religions like Taoism and Buddhism (see Sponsel and Natadecha-Sponsel in this volume). The third viewpoint is the dominant Judeo-Christian perspective which places human beings above nature and God above humans. This hierarchical ordering of nature-humans-God underpins Lynn

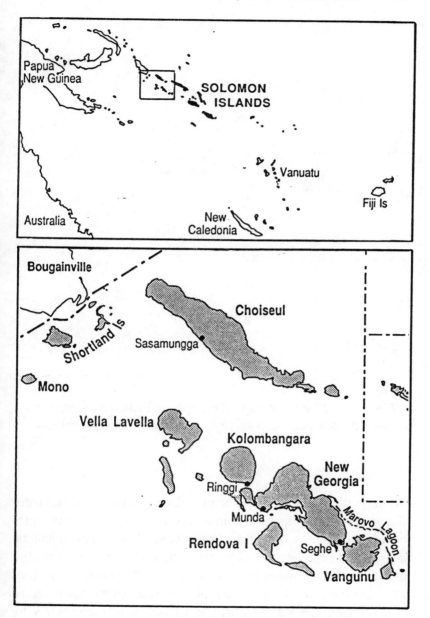

Figure 8.1. Solomon Islands location map.

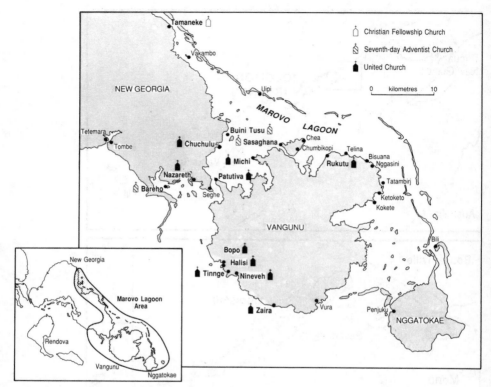

Figure 8.2. Marovo villages participating in the "environmental attitude and awareness survey" indicated by church symbols.

White's (1967) famous, but sometimes disputed, thesis that the Judeo-Christian teleology fostered human superiority over and contemptuousness of nature and thus bears blame for much of the environmental degradation experienced in Western societies. A similar conclusion may be drawn by extension of Tawney's (1926) classic work, *Religion and the Rise of Capitalism*, in which he asserts that from the Middle Ages onward the Christian Church structured society by establishing a social organization and social relations that easily evolved into an ecologically destructive capitalism. If our daily habits and actions and our science and technology are indeed dominated by values that result in our alienation from and annihilation of nature, it is easy to understand why White (1967:1206) doubts "that disastrous ecological backlash can be avoided simply by applying to our problems more science and more technology."

The results of the Marovo environmental attitude and awareness survey suggest (1) that the more traditionalistic (tribal-based) religions may well be more environmentally sustaining than introduced Christian religions; (2) that within Christianity, environmental husbandry or lack thereof appears to issue more from specific denominational precepts than from universal Christian theology; and (3) that the active participant's experience in a religion influences consciousness and attitudes toward management of natural resources; and it is this very transformative potential that offers most hope that religion may become an important vehicle for rethinking our relations with nature and with each other.

MAROVO SOCIETY

Marovo society is, perhaps, one of the most traditional, self-sufficient and autonomous in existence today. With only 10 percent of the population being cash income earners, the economy is primarily subsistence based (Solomon Islands 1989). As expected, the demographic characteristics are typical of a subsistence economy experiencing rapid population growth (approximately 4 percent per year). Alarming as this rate of growth may be, if the Marovans act on their expressed view that four children "are good for a family" in contrast to the actual five chidren per family (1987 survey data), the prospects are good for a lowering of the population growth rate in the future.

In Marovo, villages are all coastal with a population of about 150–250, and are generally comprised of a single clan group which adheres to either the Seventh-day Adventist, United Church, or Christian Fellowship faith. The majority of villagers carry the perception of an abundance of land and feel that there will be enough land for their children when they grow up. Overall, 63 percent of adult respondents surveyed answered "yes" when asked if there will be enough land for their children when they grow up. These figures are not significantly different for the Seventh-day Adventist group of villages in which 66 percent of the participants likewise feel that there will be enough land for their children.

Village social life revolves largely around food gardening and church activities (see Figure 8.3). Survey participants were asked to mark an "x" to indicate the activities they had undertaken in the A.M. and/or the P.M. on each day of the previous week. These data, as well as field observations, prove that in Marovo, religion remains a considerable force in shaping world views. As such, the role of religious institutions (indigenous or introduced) must be assessed in estimating behavioral prospects.

Pressures have emerged endogenously and exogenously to develop the considerable forest, marine, mineral, and aesthetic resources of the Marovo region. Villagers collectively own and control extensive forest and marine (lagoon) resources, both of which are being exploited largely to the benefit of non-Marovans. Resources development, actual and potential, creates conflicts among Marovans and between Marovo people and political decision-makers at different levels of Solomon Islands government.

In response to development pressures, Marovo leaders as early as May 1987 moved to approve submission of the entire Marovo Lagoon for "World Heritage Site Listing" (Minutes of Marovo Area Council Meeting, May 15, 1987). The idea has subsequently been acted on by the Solomon Islands government, through the Ministry of Tourism and Aviation, which wants to obtain World Heritage Site status for the whole of Marovo Lagoon as the basis for a sustainable rural development program. The proposal has been examined by a government-appointed consultant, and the results of a fact-finding mission have been published. The report indicates:

> The Ministry is strongly in favor of pursuing World Heritage Site Listing because of the prestige it would bring and the exposure it will give to the Solomon Islands as a tourist destination. Listing would

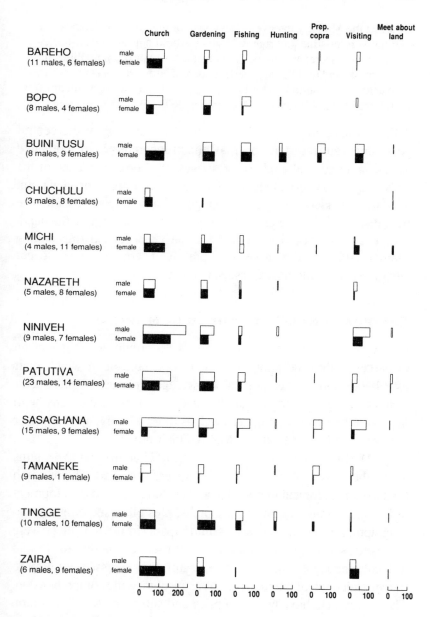

Figure 8.3.   Marovo adult activity frequency during the week prior to the field survey in June – July 1987. (The width of each bar represents the total number of times each activity had been undertaken.)

assist the Ministry to develop an image of the Solomon Islands as a relatively pristine environment which would appeal to well-heeled apologists and enable associated businesses to develop facilities for the upper and middle range segments of the tourist market in which particular attention can be paid to special nature tours, sometimes referred to as soft tourism (McKinnon 1990:36).

Although support for World Heritage Site Listing by the central government and the Marovo Area Council apparently is not motivated by the same general goals or principles, the correspondence of the ends sought may serve to legitimize the proposal from the viewpoint of Marovo leaders and the national politicians supportive of it. The final disposition of the proposal will, however, depend on the depth and breadth of popular support for the proposal existing among Marovo villagers. The survey data presented here allow us to speculate on some problems and issues that may arise.

ENVIRONMENTAL ATTITUDES IN MAROVO

Marovans are aware of the impacts of economic development on resources within the continuum of lagoon land upon which their livelihoods and their ecological knowledge are based. This conclusion is based on formal surveys and informal discussions with Marovans of all social status, as well as those who live in Marovo or who work in Honiara but call Marovo their home.

During July 1987, 375 individuals (223 adults and 152 youths above the age of 14) from 14 villages were surveyed. The research focused on ecological knowledge and attitudes toward development of local, communally owned resources, plus other sociological, demographic, and economic factors. Participants from each village were surveyed as a group, and a translator was used for English and Pidgin to local languages. Questions were carefully expressed not only to prevent injection of bias but also to ensure clarity and comprehension. The survey data have been compiled and submitted to the Solomon Islands Ministry of Natural Resources, and the results presented here are only those appropriate to the argument being advanced.

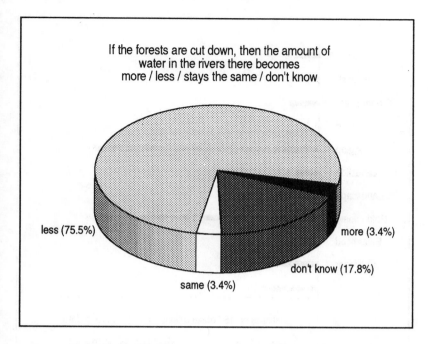

If the forests are cut down, then the amount of
water in the rivers there becomes
more / less / stays the same / don't know

less (75.5%)

more (3.4%)

don't know (17.8%)

same (3.4%)

Figure 8.4. Marovan's perception of the impact of forest removal
on the quantity of water in local rivers (data combined for all
villages; 208 respondents).

An example of Marovans' ecological knowledge is presented
in Figures 8.4 and 8.5. The ecological significance of the pattern
shown in Figure 8.4 is the overwhelming perception that removal of
forests will have a negative impact on the amount of water in local
rivers. It is important to mention here that villagers depend on nearby
rivers to meet all of their water needs. Figure 8.5 highlights attitudes
toward mining and logging activities in an area where lagoon resources are as essential to livelihood as those of the land. Since mining
or logging activities have not yet been established within Marovo
proper, the activities that "cause the water in the lagoon to get bad"

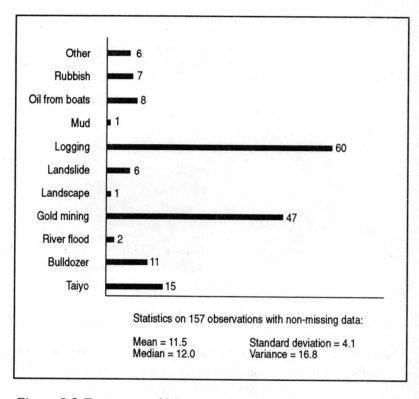

Figure 8.5. Frequency of Marovan perception of sources of lagoon
water pollution.

indicate the concerns that will play a role in future decisions over
mining or logging on village-owned lands.

The villagers' attitudes toward resources development are
illustrated in the responses to questions concerning logging and
tourism (see Figures 8.6 and 8.7). The results are shown by church
affiliation. Seventh-day Adventist villagers are much more supportive of potential economic development activities than villagers of the
United Church or the Christian Fellowship denominations. Despite

the differences in sample sizes, the consistency of the variation in the responses to questions pertaining to logging and development of tourism highlights the potentially significant role of religious philosophy in shaping resource-development decisions in the Pacific.

The relationship between Christian denominations and attitude toward economic development is an entirely unanticipated aspect of this research. Nonetheless, there is widespread perception among Marovans that fundamental differences exist in attitudes between villages, and anecdotal evidence relates this to Christian denominational affiliation. (This observation has provided impetus for the inquiry presented in this paper.) The expressed differences in attitude toward development, if at all predictive of behavior, are bound to

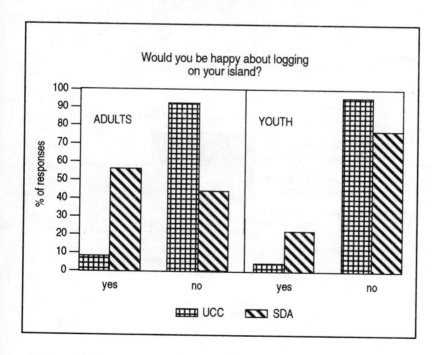

Figure 8.6. Attitudes toward logging on clan or village lands expressed by adults and youth in United Church and Seventh-day Adventist villages.

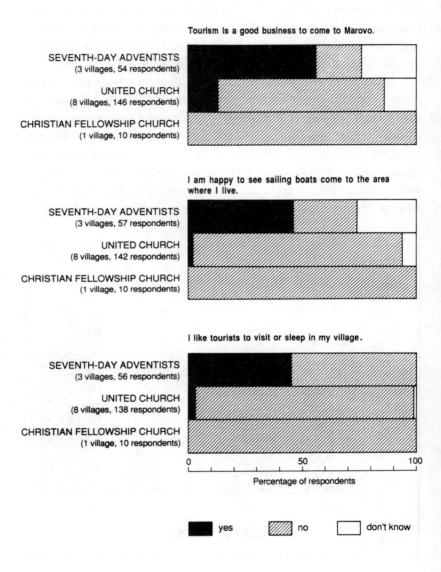

Figure 8.7. Marovan's attitudes toward various aspects of tourism development in relation to Christian denominational affiliation.

present barriers to community acceptance of World Heritage Site Listing for the entire Marovo Lagoon, and are also portentous of intraregional conflict.

Much insight into the religious foundations of environmental attitudes can be gained by examining the world views of the Christian denominations present in Marovo and by speculating on the influence of religious doctrine on environmental attitudes. In so doing the responses to the survey may be better contextualized, allowing the results to be judged in respect of their implications for sustainability of Marovo culture and ecology.

RELIGION AND ENVIRONMENT IN MAROVO

In Marovo, not unlike the rest of Solomon Islands, Christianity is pervasive and influential. Marovo villages are unidenominational and staunchly faithful. Of the 56 villages in the Western Province's Marovo ward (which is an area extending beyond the lagoon), 35 villages are Seventh-day Adventist, 18 United Church, and 3 subscribe to the Christian Fellowship Church. However, the relatively late arrival of Christianity in Marovo in the second decade of the twentieth century, the geographical isolation, and the high degree of local self-sufficiency allow us to accept that certain customary beliefs and practices persist as significant interacting variables impacting on individual thought and action across Christian denominational affiliation (see Finau and Garrett 1973). Hviding (1988) confirms that Christianity, in Marovo society exhibits many syncretic elements and that this applies not just to the endemic and strongly traditionalistic Christian Fellowship Church but to all denominations.

Pacific anthropologists and historians (such as Keesing 1978, Laracy 1983, and contributors to Jolly and MacIntyre 1989) have illustrated why the growth and importance of Christian missions should not be neglected by anyone who wants to understand the attitudes and values that have shaped past events and will influence future choices in the Pacific. Hannett (1970) makes the important observation that for a long time in the history of formal education in Papua New Guinea, the Christian churches pioneered in this field. This is generally true for Melanesia as a whole. Hannett (1970:655) further said: "So great a role did the Christian churches play in development that even in some areas, the churches have been the government in action." Since the Christian churches and not colonial administrations pioneered in most areas of social development in the contemporary Pacific, environmental attitudes are more reflective of church/religious precepts rather than political ones in many parts of the Pacific.

The extremely powerful influence exerted by the churches in Pacific social development is inarguable. However, that fact does not necessarily imply that religion always assumes causal primacy in actions and their outcomes. We must remember what the geographer-metaphysician Yi-Fu Tuan (1974:245) has written: "A person is a biological organism, a social being and a unique individual; perceptions, attitudes and values reflect all three levels of being." The accounts of indigenous religious movements in the Pacific by Laracy (1983) and the contributors to Loeliger and Trompf (1985) provide ample support for Tuan's argument. This tension between introduced religious doctrine and self-actualizing individuals is conveyed by Keesing's (1989:209) assessment of social unrest among the bush Kwaio of Malaita (Solomon Islands). Keesing finds that "the struggle between Christian and 'heathen' cannot be viewed as one theology doing battle with another, but must be understood as a deeper and more subtle and complex struggle for political domination and with the power to define what [their] culture is to be." Kwaio unrest and the accounts of other so-called nativistic religious movements in the Pacific underscore the multiple dimensionality of social reality, alerting us that individual volition opens up the possibility of unity, opposition, and contradiction in our observations (Soja 1989).

The survey reported here amply corroborates Soja's position. Nonetheless the results imply that at present, in parts of Solomon Islands, religion remains a considerable force in shaping world views, and, specifically, attitudes toward the utilization and preservation of resources. Moreover, the results demonstrate the critical importance of specific denominational precepts in shaping human consciousness, decisions, and actions. Yet the results also indicate that although it is most influential, faithful adherence to religious dogma produces contradictions that are reflected in the ambivalence shown in some responses obtained in the survey. For example, all but 1 out of 298 villagers say that it is still important to know *the ways of kastom* (custom) although conversion to Christianity has, to varying degrees, required the renunciation of customary religious beliefs.

     To explore how the three Christian denominations – Seventh-day Adventist, United Church, and the Christian Fellowship Church – present in Marovo Lagoon may produce quite different environmental attitudes, we must first examine those tenets of each faith that may variously influence people's perceptions of nature and their relationship to the natural world.

The Seventh-day Adventists

The Seventh-day Adventist church is the fifth largest mission in the Solomon Islands claiming nearly 29,000 members in 1986, close to 50 percent of whom are concentrated in the Western Province. Seventh-day Adventist membership increased by more than 90 percent between 1970 and 1986, making it the fastest-growing Christian mission in Solomon Islands. Much of this growth has taken place in Marovo where approximately 60 percent of the population are Seventh-day Adventists, with the United Church claiming most of the remainder of the population (Solomon Islands 1989:174).

     The works of historians Damsteegt (1977), Patrick (1986), Hilliard (1966, 1978), and Steley (1983 and pers. com.) provide a solid base of information on Seventh-day Adventism in general and, more particularly, Seventh-day Adventist missions in the Pacific. Hilliard and Steley have written specifically about the Adventist mission in the Solomon Islands. Collectively, these sources, together with personal interviews of Seventh-day Adventists, have greatly contributed to the understanding of Adventism presented here.

Adventism is guided by a theology and lifestyle comprised of clear-cut beliefs and rigid behavioral demands which set its adherents apart from other Christians, thereby causing them to become socially estranged from the rest of society (Steley 1983). It appears certain that Adventism's general world view, together with its organizational strategy stressing unity, uniformity, and separation of its members from nonmembers, has contributed greatly to the success of the mission in the Solomon Islands. These same strategies could be an effective means of promoting particularisms manifested in attitudes toward nature and management of natural resources.

The following discussion shows how blind adherence to Church orthodoxy, constructive of a world view and a corporatist management system, may foster separatism and superiority, and may predispose Seventh-day Adventists toward culpable apathy and inaction in the sphere of resources management in their local region, nation, and the world.

Adventist World View. Individualism, remnantism, eschatology, and millenarianism are fundamental tenets of Seventh-day Adventist belief system. Seventh-day Adventism, more than any of the other denominations present in Marovo, gives credence to Glacken's (1967:150) observation that the "intense other-worldliness and rejection of the beauties of nature because they turn man away from the contemplation of God are elaborated upon far more in theological writings than in the Bible itself."

A proper construction of Adventist world view, in the context of the Pacific, requires a brief ontological review. Adventist missionaries to the Pacific (first to Australia and then to the Solomon Islands) left the United States in the 1890s. This was a time when European migrants poured into the United States to partake of the American dream. Likewise, others around the world were mesmerized by achievements within American society, interpreting them "as God's handiwork" (Damsteegt 1977:7). Likewise, Patrick (1986:19) has remarked, it is "impossible to consider the Australian [and Solomon

Islands] arm of the Seventh-day Adventist Church in isolation from its North American head." Reflecting their American origins, Adventist missionaries to the Pacific carried with them democratic and individualistic ideals and a Christianity characterized by a millennial consciousness and a utilitarian attitude toward natural resources (Damsteegt 1977:7). Promotion of individualism and focus on self works against responsible resources management as it promotes "man"-nature dualism and conditions people to ignore the ecological implications of their actions. A society in which individualism is democratically acted upon leads inexorably to the "tragedy of the commons" (Hardin 1968). Still, this is of little consequence if one does not anticipate a future in this world. Adventism does not anticipate a future in this world. Its theology promises that with the parousia, or second coming of Christ, Adventists will inherit a New Jerusalem which will see the dissolution of the earth and the renovation of nature (Damstgeet 1977:30).

Eschatology – the belief in the imminence of judgment day, which is yet another fundamental tenet of the Adventist belief system – is based on the apocalyptic literature of the Old and New Testaments as, for example, "the command 'Babylon has fallen ... come out of her my people' which became a vocal part of Seventh-day Adventists theology of mission" (Steley 1983:3). This millenarian theology is accompanied by the conviction that Adventists are the "little remnant" people (i.e., God's true church) chosen to proclaim the last warning message to the world in a wicked and adulterous end-time (Damsteegt 1977; Patrick 1986). How, then, must a select remnant people perceive of their role and responsibility toward social problems in general and, in particular, the principles underlying the concept of cultural and ecological sustainability? Patrick (1986:21) offers that against the cataclysmic backdrop of the Adventists' world: "Social concerns seemed worth little contention. And in any case, no ultimate good would be achieved even by just laws ... since depravity in all its forms could be cured only by spiritual regeneration."

In addition to its eschatological emphasis and separatist posture toward the wider society, Seventh-day Adventism prescribes that its followers assume particular attitudinal stances for specific situations (see Hoekema 1963). For instance, Seventh-day Adventist's emphasis on individual appearances of progress fosters a transformationist ethic. Their laws prohibit members from engaging in social action or even making apparent their prejudices for or against political matters. So, in dictating social behaviors, Adventist theology makes, or attempts to make, religion a "full-time, whole life experience" (Steley, pers. com.). The aim is to manifest the lived world of the "remnant people"; and effectively cut off adherents from close association with all but those of their own religion (Steley 1983:14).

The overall impact of Adventist theological precepts on Solomon Islands society has been assessed by both Hilliard and Steley. Steley (1983:106), himself an Adventist, argues that because Adventism requires that converts *substitute* the Adventist world view for their customary way of life, Adventist converts distance themselves more from their former culture and religion than do converts to other Christian missions. In justification of the Adventist "package deal" approach, Steley (1983:131) asserts: "Drastic as the S.D.A. sponsored culture change may have seemed, it is possible that it was the best way of bringing Solomon Islanders into a happy relationship with the modern world."

In a real sense Adventism with its embrace of democracy, entrepreneurialism, and motivation toward better material living might well have been sufficient remedy to much, if not all, of the social ills that recent nativistic religious movements (like the Christian Fellowship Church) generally sought to redress. Hilliard (1966:426) seems to concur when he states: "To the islanders Seventh-day Adventism appeared less a set of doctrines than a new and binding way of life." Unfortunately, a way of life characterized by millenarian theology, other worldliness, materialism, prohibition against political action, and blind obedience to civil government may not offer much hope for the emergence of an ethic for creating authentically sustainable social and ecological relations.

The United (Methodist) Church

The United Church resulted from the union, in the 1960s, of various Protestant (including Methodist) denominations within Solomon Islands and other South Pacific countries. From 1902 until 1916 (when the first Seventh-day Adventists mission was established at Sasaghana Village, Marovo Island), Methodists were the dominant Christian group in the Roviana district (which is an area that includes Marovo Lagoon and New Georgia Island) (refer to Figure 8.2). In Marovo proper, the first Methodist mission was established at Patutiva Village in 1912.

But the Methodist mission did not achieve wholesale conversion of Marovo villagers. Instead some Marovo villagers chose to convert to other denominations such as the Church of England whose missionaries were known to offer an opportunity to learn the English language (Hviding 1988:36). This rationale illustrates how islanders assessed the impact of imported cultures in terms of contributions to their personal and social goals (Boutilier 1978). They actively pursue mission groups that show promise for tangible gain. Thus the persistence of unconverted villages and some resentment toward individual Methodist missionaries made it possible for the Adventists to gain entry to the Marovo mission field.

With the establishment of the Adventist mission, the Methodists lost hegemony within Roviana such that by 1986 the number of Methodists in Marovo was second to Adventists.

The United (Methodist) Church's loss of dominance in Marovo and its present slowing rate of growth (Solomon Islands 1989) can be attributed to the following: (1) the tenets of Methodism were cast in a more liberal theology than Adventism; (2) the Methodist's mission, unlike the Adventists', was less egalitarian, less didactic, and consequently less culturally alienating; and (3) the means by which the Methodist Church could be used as a vehicle for achieving personal material improvement were less apparent than for its Adventist competitor.

Methodist World View. Davies (1963:184) has said that at its core Methodism strives for personal holiness and for the redemption of society as a whole. Thus, in addition to its aim of winning humankind from a life of sin, Methodism aims to help promote social and humanitarian reform. Bett (1937:210) notes that its founder John Wesley "had no social theories of an original or revolutionary kind to propound, and he possessed no supernatural provision of the social development of the next century." Strict behavioral dictates were not laid down by John Wesley whose theology was not shaped by visions and apparitions as was those of Ellen White who articulated much of Seventh-day Adventist doctrine. Consequently Methodists' behavior was to be guided simply by temperance, not prohibition.

Within the latitude offered by such a liberal reformist theology, Methodist missionaries to Solomon Islands could rationalize their own ideals of social relationships and relations of production. In these two spheres, missionary John Francis Goldie, an Australian who established the first Methodist mission at Roviana, stands out as having played the pivotal role in shaping the history of the mission. Goldie was the mission. He exerted considerable influence in the region well into the 1950s and may bear some responsibility for the fortunes and misfortunes of his church in Roviana. Scholars have generally cast Goldie as an aggressive and, unfortunately, abrasive personality who was by inclination "a man of affairs rather than a scholar or a pastor of souls" (Hilliard 1966:248). Goldie enthusiastically embarked on an "industrial program," primarily involving production and trading of copra, designed to benefit the mission financially and to bestow the protestant work ethic (Steley 1983).

Scholars now believe that Goldie's industrial program created conflict with other local planters and contributed to the loss of the Methodist monopoly in Roviana (Hilliard 1966:253). In addition, disenchantment grew over the less than egalitarian structure of social relationship that existed between missionary and flock. The emergence of unequal social relations between missionary and flock is sharply conveyed by Harwood (1978:237), who says "Goldie had nothing but scorn for islanders who attempted to emulate the life-style of the European missionaries." She evidences this conclusion by reference to Reverend Goldie's remarks about the

> religious loafer ... the half-civilized native who loves to strut round quoting passages of the Bible singing hymns, and shaking hands in the slightest provocation, but who has learned nothing of industry, honesty or cleanliness. ... He has been taught the Christian creed divorced from Christian conduct. He, too, is ready to "preach the gospel, not to work," but, unlike our white friend, he is to be pitied more than blamed.

But if, as Tawney (1926) suggests, "Christian conduct" implies the Protestant work ethic, it may not be wrong to say that a foremost reason for the erosion of Methodist legitimacy was its failure to disseminate among villagers the requisite means of production and/or entrepreneurship so that they too might partake of that materiality, which to Islanders might have been the essential difference between missionary and convert. In this regard, it is enlightening to consider one islander's lament as reported in Laracy's (1983:14) study of the Solomon Islands' "Maasiña Rule" (brotherhood) movement: "We have only been taught the gospel, but nothing yet about trade or commerce." Here it is clearly revealed why, ethically, one prerequisite for ecological sustainability should be economic development toward better material conditions of life for those who do not already partake in the feast of material life. This perspective is firmly articulated by Miskaram (1985) who says that, in the main, what is often being sought by Melanesians and expressed in new politico-religious movements is a material solution to the ideological expression of unequal development. This message is now being purveyed by a number of writers (cf. World Commission on Environment and Development 1987); but who has heard it?

One assumption that can be made from the foregoing discussion and the survey results is that the loosely articulated religion purveyed by Methodist missionaries is only weakly integrated into the fabric of Solomon Islands culture. Consequently, Williams (1970:677) suggests that conversion may have resulted only in the adoption of Christianity – with its promise of material rewards, but "the way in which they related Christ to their culture remained unchanged and was along the lines of the old animistic religion. ... In reality what resulted was a culture transformed only in outward form."

Hilliard (1966:6) notes that traditional Solomon Islands religion was an essentially materialistic religion and concurs with Meggitt (1965:18) that the traditional religion was a "technology rather than a spiritual force for human salvation." The animistic beliefs and practices integrated the total life of society, providing, says Keesing (1989:212), "its main ritual dramas"; guardian of food and forest resources; and creating "the invisible lines and invisible but powerful ancestral ghosts that imposed and policed them."

By accepting that features of the customary religion persist in Methodist villages to a far greater extent than in Seventh-day Adventist villages, it may be hypothesized that any significant difference in environmental attitudes between Methodists and Adventists is a measure of the degree of penetration and cultural alienation created by the foreign religions. Hence, Methodist missionaries, by allowing greater ad hoc selection and blending of doctrine than the Adventists, allowed for the emergence of attitudes and values more closely akin to those held by the most traditionalistic of the three religious denominations: the Christian Fellowship Church.

The Christian Fellowship Church

> I suppose one has to pity the missionaries because while they tried to bring us the pure milk of the Gospel they found it hard to free themselves from the cultural, emotional and social frame in which they were accustomed to live and express themselves. Because of this Christianity has become unwittingly an enemy of nationalism. For our culture is essentially a religious culture. Our customs and behavior therefore are geared to religious concepts and the missionaries in trying to convert us to new religions could not escape condemning our culture (Hannett 1970).

Although Hannett's comments are in reference to Papua New Guinea, he captures one of the fundamental grievances that the so-called "nativist movements" in Solomon Islands (Christian Fellowship Church, Maasiña Rule, and the Remnant Church, among others) have sought to express. Thus historians have claimed that the Christian Fellowship Church "was as much a rejection of the colonial relationship in the west as Maasiña Rule in the east" (Bennett 1987:310). Maasiña Rule (literally translated as Marching Rule) was a post–World War II movement which united much of the island of Malaita against the British Protectorate Government. Of Maasiña Rule, Keesing (1973:29) had the following to say:

> It was *not* primarily a "Cargo Cult"; it was *not* primarily a form of oppressive demagoguery or dictatorship. It was an amazingly sophisticated political and social movement aimed at transcending tribal fragmentation, transforming society from the ground up, and presenting a united front against colonial oppression.

The Christian Fellowship Church, officially established in 1961, was the result of a breakaway movement within the Methodist mission at Roviana. The leader of the breakaway group of Methodists was the charismatic and eccentric Melanesian Silas Eto, who became known to his followers as the "Holy Mama." Harwood (1971, 1978), who has extensively studied the movement that led to the establishment of the Christian Fellowship Movement, states that "the controversies which culminated in the breakaway resulted in a claim on the part of the Christian Fellowship Church to represent the *true* Methodist church in the Solomons" (Harwood 1978:232). Tuza (1970, 1975) attributes the rise of the Christian Fellowship Church to the failure to indigenize local Christian worship. In attempting to explain Eto's action and the subsequent success of his church, Harwood further notes that despite the longstanding contact and interaction of missionaries and Melanesians there was a failure to establish a shared set of cognitions, motivations, and goals. As a result, there emerged only "partial equivalent structures" or a limited degree of cultural understanding which only retarded accommodation by the Melanesians for whom "social equivalence is a dominant theme" in political thought (Harwood 1978:240). After over four decades of close association with Methodist missionaries in Roviana, Eto was well positioned between mission and sect to adapt Methodism to the set of cognitions, motivations, and goals held by other disaffected mission converts. The religion became a strong assertion of Solomon Islands' consciousness because it was "highly emotional in form but strongly indigenous in leadership, worship, and all facets of its life" (Williams 1970:672).

Once established, the Christian Fellowship Church spread rapidly throughout Roviana and some of the smaller islands nearby (Tippett 1967). Eto's church has been described as "thoroughly syncretic – incorporating Methodist and Roman Catholic beliefs with pre-Christian magical rites, behavior and belief" (Tippett 1967:212). Attitudes toward the natural world expressed by members of the Christian Fellowship Church parallel beliefs held by the similarly syncretic Remnant Church that sprung up on Malaita in the late 1950s. As part of its philosophy concerning creation, "Remnantists believe that God's whole creation is perfect. ... Therefore unnecessary exploitation of God's creation is as bad as disobeying God himself" (Maetoloa 1985).

At present, villagers belonging to the Christian Fellowship Church are staunchly traditionalistic, stressing self-sufficiency through community enterprises, communalism, and reciprocity. It should not be surprising that the Christian Fellowship Church, or any church, has a strong entrepreneurial dimension since this is foundational to a secure future. A further and crucial aspect of the nativistic Christian Fellowship Church is that it provides members the opportunity to reconstruct their Melanesian dignity and regain cultural pride which experienced strong deconstructive pressures since European contact.

We hope that the high degree of environmental awareness, reciprocity, humility *in* nature, and overall utopianism expressed by Christian Fellowship Church members interviewed during the survey is reflective of an ecological meaning system firmly owned and lived by all adherents of the Christian Fellowship Church.

Environmental attitudes expressed by Christian Fellowship Church members reflect knowledge that binds, creating a heightened sense of belonging and "placeness" (Relph 1976). Attachment to place is important, if not requisite, to the development of understanding and praxis of "authentic" ecologically sustainable development. Furthermore, intimacy with the land, besides causing place to become sacralized, forces deep understanding of the nature of individual dependence on and responsibility for the proper maintenance of place. Tuan (1977:152) tells us why this is so:

> Religions of this local type encourage in their devotees a strong sense of the past, of lineage and continuity in place. ... Security is gained through this historical sense of continuity rather than by the light of eternal timeless values as propounded in transcendental and universal religions.

Over the years membership in the Christian Fellowship Church has experienced a high rate of growth, increasing by more than 81 percent between 1970 and 1986. However, after nearly three decades the church remains concentrated in the Western Province where 94 percent of its total membership of just over 7,000 are located (Solomon Islands 1989). The failure of the Christian Fellowship Church to diffuse more widely throughout the country may reflect its lack of universal appeal in a modernizing Solomon Islands. It may also reflect the impact of cultural boundaries within the country itself, as well as the strength of other Christian denominations.

CONCLUSION

In situations as found in Marovo where firm belief in God and attendant values dominate culture, religious precepts strongly influence attitudes toward nature. Specifically, religious beliefs that influence people's posture toward resources use are conceptions about the future and actions and inactions motivated by such beliefs. The important consideration here is whether religious dogma subscribes to long-term or short-term views of the future. For if there is a limit to the future, such as found in "the end is near" philosophy, actions taken to secure an ecologically sustainable future may well be heterodox to church precepts.

A short-term view of life easily promotes individualistic and utilitarian attitudes and exploitative relations with nature. The opposite view is the belief in a long-term future – a continuation of all life with the awakening of life's endless potentialities – and an accompanying sense of responsibility to engage in sustaining relationships with the natural world, if not for nature's sake, then for the reason that one's life endures through one's progeny. A philosophy that supports a long-term view of all creation fosters attitudes not unlike those encoded in many animistic/traditional religions wherein each individual is an integral part of creation and all nature like all peoples are sanctified, worthy of reverence and protection.

Although the discussion in this paper has placed emphasis on a single influential factor underlying the divergence in attitudes toward resources development in Marovo, other causalities (e.g., political or geographic) are not being dismissed. In addition, although the responses to the survey allow attitudes to be differentiated along denominational lines, the responses can also be seen as representing a continuum of views. No village is entirely in opposition to the next. Thus although influential, Christian denominational precepts may not be determinant. Despite the overlay of religious philosophy, Marovans are clearly aware of their role and responsibility in maintaining the natural base of their sustenance. This knowledge provides hope that the great potential for authentic ecological sustainability in Marovo may be achieved.

REFERENCES

Bennett, J. A. 1987. *Wealth of the Solomons: A History of a Pacific Archipelago, 1800–1978*. Pacific Islands Monograph No. 3. Honolulu, HI: University of Hawai'i Press.

Bett, H. 1937. *The Spirit of Methodism.* London: Epworth Press.

Boutilier, J. A. 1978. "Missions, Administration, and Education in the Solomon Islands, 1893–1942," in J. A. Boutilier, D. T. Hughes, and S. W. Tiffany, eds., *Mission, Church and Sect in Oceania.* ASAO Monograph No. 6. Ann Arbor: University of Michigan Press.

Damsteegt, P. G. 1977. *Foundations of the Seventh-day Adventist Message and Mission.* Grand Rapids, MI: William B. Eardmans Publishing.

Davies, R. 1963. *Methodism.* London: Penguin.

Finau, P., and J. Garrett. 1973. "Future of Religious Regionalism." *Pacific Perspective* 11(1): 42–48.

Glacken, Clarence J. 1967. *Traces on the Rhodean Shore.* Berkeley, CA: University of California Press.

Goulet, D. 1990. "Development Ethics and Ecological Wisdom," in J. Ronald Engels and Joan Gibb Engels, *Ethics of Environment and Development.* London: Belhaven Press.

Hannett, L. 1970. "The Church and Nationalism," in M. W. Ward, ed., *The Politics of Melanesia.* Pp. 654–665. Australian National University Research School of Pacific Studies, Canberra, and University of Papua New Guinea, Port Moresby.

Hardin, G. 1968. "The Tragedy of the Commons." *Science* 162:1243–1248.

Harwood, F. H. 1971. "The Christian Fellowship Church: A Revitalization Movement in Melanesia. PhD diss., University of Chicago.

Harwood, F. H. 1978. "Intercultural Communication in the Western Solomons: The Methodist Mission and the Emergence of the Christian Fellowship Church," in J. A. Boutilier, D. T. Hughes, and S. W. Tiffany, eds., *Mission, Church and Sect in Oceania.* ASAO Monograph No. 6. Ann Arbor: University of Michigan Press.

Hilliard, D. L. 1966. Protestant Missions in the Solomon Islands, 1849–1942. 2 vols. PhD diss., Australian National University, Canberra.

Hilliard, D. 1978. *God's Gentlemen.* St. Lucia: University of Queensland Press.

Hoekema, A. A. 1963. *Seventh-day Adventism.* Grand Rapids, MI: William B. Eardmans Publishing.

Hviding, E. 1988. Sharing Paths and Keeping Sides: Managing the Sea in Marovo Lagoon, Solomon Islands. Thesis, Department of Anthropology, University of Bergen, Norway.

Jolly, M., and M. MacIntyre. 1989. *Family and Gender in the Pacific.* London: Cambridge University Press.

Keesing, R. 1973. "Seeking Paths for Solomons' Development." *Pacific Perspective* 2(1):21–34.

Keesing, R. 1978. "Politico-Religious Movements and Anti-colonialism on Malaita: Maasiña Rule in Historical Perspective, Part 1." *Oceania* 48(4): 241–261.

Keesing, R. 1989. "Sins of a Mission: Christian Life as Kwaio Traditionalist Ideology," in M. Jolly and M. MacIntyre, eds., *Family and Gender in the Pacific*. Pp. 193–212. London: Cambridge University Press.

Laracy, H., ed. 1983. *The Maasiña Rule Movement, Solomon Islands, 1944–1952*. Institute of Pacific Studies, University of the South Pacific, Suva.

Leopold, A. 1949. *A Sandy County Almanac*. New York: Oxford University Press.

Loeliger, C., and G. Trompf, eds. 1985. *New Religious Movements in Melanesia*. University of the South Pacific, Suva, and University of Papua New Guinea, Port Moresby.

Maetoloa, M. 1985. "The Remnant Church," in C. Loeliger and G. Trompf, eds., *New Religious Movements in Melanesia*. Pp. 120–148. University of the South Pacific, Suva, and University of Papua New Guinea, Port Moresby.

Malo, D. 1951. *Hawaiian Antiquities*. Translated by Nathaniel Emerson, 1898. Honolulu, HI: Bernice P. Bishop Museum.

Martin, C. 1978. *Keepers of the Game: Indian-Animal Relationships and the Fur Trade*. Berkeley, CA: University of California Press.

McKinnon, J. 1990. Solomon Islands World Heritage Site Proposal: Fact Finding Mission (4–22 February 1990). Department of Geography, University of Wellington, New Zealand.

Meggitt, J. M. 1965. *The Lineage System of the Mae-Enga of New Guinea*. Edinburgh: Oliver and Boyd.

Miskaram, N. 1985. "Cargo Cultism on New Hanover: A Psychological Phenomenon or an Indication of Unequal Development?" in C. Loeliger and G. Trompf, eds., *New Religious Movements in Melanesia*. Pp. 75–89. University of South Pacific, Suva, and University of Papua New Guinea, Port Moresby.

Patrick, N. 1986. "Doctrine and Deed: Adventism's Encounter with Its Society in Nineteenth-Century Australia," in A. J. Ferch, ed., *Symposium on Adventist History in the South Pacific: 1885–1918*. Pp. 19–29. Wahroonga, NSW, Australia: South Pacific Division of Seventh-day Adventists.

Relph, E. 1976. *Place and Placeness*. London: Pion.

Soja, E. 1989. *Postmodern Geographies*. New York: Verso.

Solomon Islands. 1989. *Report on the Census of Population 1986: Report 2-B Data Analysis*. Honiara: Ministry of Finance.

Steley, D. 1983. Juapa Rane: Seventh-day Adventist Mission in the Solomon Islands, 1914–1942. MA thesis, University of Auckland, New Zealand.

Tawny, R. H. 1926. *Religion and the Rise of Capitalism.* London: John Murray.

Tippett, A. R. 1967. *Solomon Islands Christianity.* London: Lutterworth Press.

Tuan, Yi-Fu. 1974. *Topophilia.* New Jersey: Prentice-Hall.

Tuan, Yi-Fu. 1977. *Space and Place.* Minneapolis: University of Minnesota Press.

Tuza, E. T. 1970. Towards Indigenization of Christian Worship in the Western Solomons. Thesis (B. Divinity), Pacific Theological College, Suva.

Tuza, E. T. 1975. The Emergence of the Christian Fellowship Church: A Historical View of Silas Eto, Founder of the Christian Fellowship Church. MA Thesis, University of Papua New Guinea.

Valeri, V. 1985. *Kinship and Sacrifice.* Chicago: University of Chicago Press.

White, L., Jr. 1967. "The Historical Roots of Our Ecological Crisis." *Science* 155:1203–1207.

Williams, R. G. 1970. "From Mission to Church: A Study of the United Church," in M. W. Ward, ed., *The Politics of Melanesia.* Pp. 666–680. Australian National University Research School of Pacific Studies, Canberra, and University of Papua New Guinea, Port Moresby.

World Commission on Environment and Development. 1987. *Our Common Future.* New York: Oxford University Press.

Chapter 9

TRADITIONAL NATIVE HAWAIIAN ENVIRONMENTAL PHILOSOPHY

Michael Kioni Dudley

A FISH STORY

If one meets a Hawaiian fisherman loading his nets and gear into his truck, he never asks if the man is going fishing. He might ask if the man is going *holoholo* (out for a ride) or he might ask if he is going to the mountains. But if he asks if the man is going fishing, the man will remove his gear out of the truck, and that will be the end of fishing for the day. For the fish will "hear" and know that the fisherman is coming, and they won't be there when he gets to the sea.

One also hears that senior Hawaiians are sometimes observed talking to plants and trees before picking their flowers – asking before taking – and that they often leave offerings when they take something of significance.

Many Hawaiians also believe that they have ancestral spirits (*'aumakua*) who dwell in animal or other nature forms. Among these are the *mo'o* (lizards), various birds and fish, rainbows, various cloud forms, forests, and mountains. Perhaps the best known of the ancestral spirits is Pele, the goddess who dwells in Kilauea volcano. Pele, in her lava form, flows down among the people on occasion. Hawaiians know the nature forms to which their families are related. They think of their ancestral spirits and the nature forms they inhabit as family members. When they encounter their *'aumakua*, they recognize the occurrence as special: a greeting, or possibly a warning, or an affirmation of the correctness of some action.

Actions such as these certainly reflect a different world view. In ancient *Hawai'i*, humans, gods, and nature formed a consciously interacting and interrelating cosmic community. All the species of nature were thought to be sentient – capable of knowing, choosing, and acting. Through evolution, all were related as kin. Hawaiians lived in a community in which humans, gods, and nature cared for one another and watched over and protected one another as family. There were rules to be observed in the community with nature – environmental ethics. Humans were expected to do their part, and the gods and nature were expected to respond. A reciprocation from any of the three required its own reciprocation in return.

The world today runs according to the Western person's perspective. That perspective treats nature as a commodity, as scientifically measurable forces, and as resources to be used, rather than as fellow beings in an interrelating world community.

What doesn't correspond with a Western person's world view is seen as of little value and as something that can and probably should be ignored. But an approach to life developed over thousands of years must contain much wisdom. During the two millennia that Hawaiian people lived in these islands, they developed a complete and unique system of thought. This explained their world and how things in it interrelated with one another, and also how people fit into the complete picture. Like the Indians, Chinese, Japanese, American Indians, and others, Hawaiians approached the world from a distinctively non-Western perspective. This Hawaiian perspective or world view formed the basis for a philosophical tradition which, although very different from the modern Western view, does explain the world just as adequately. One can function in today's world while approaching it from the traditional Hawaiian-thought framework just as well as one can by approaching it from the Western-thought framework. Certainly, for island dwellers, there must be special insights and wisdom in the Hawaiian approach.

MATTER AND SPIRIT IN EVOLUTIONARY THEORY

In Hawaiian thought, there are close parallels between humans and nature. Hawaiians traditionally have viewed the entire world as being alive in the same way that humans are alive. They have thought *all* of nature as conscious – able to know and to act – and able to interrelate with humans. The Hawaiians had a quite elaborately worked out theory of evolution: its ascent of species, as told in the famous chant *Kumulipo*, corresponds surprisingly well with Darwinian theory. The *Kumulipo* speaks of spirit as well as matter: in contrast to Judeo-Christian thought, it presents both matter and spirit as existing in the beginning, existing quite separately. In further contrast to Western thought, *both* matter and spirit are seen to be conscious, if we define "conscious" as active, knowledgeable, able to make choices, and able to reduce will to action. As evolution progressed, spirit inhabited the various material species, so that they seem to have both material consciousness and spiritual consciousness. Nature, like humans, then, had the conscious ability to know and to act, to watch over, to protect, and to interrelate with humans. Humans, who stood at the top of the evolutionary ladder, formed a continuum of consciousness with nature beneath them, in sharp contrast with Western thought where humans are the anomaly, the only beings who think.

Hawaiians also viewed the land, the sky, the sea, and all the other species of nature preceding them as family – as conscious ancestral beings who had evolved earlier on the evolutionary ladder, who cared for and protected humans, and who deserved similar treatment (*aloha 'aina* [love for the land]) in return.

THE ROLE OF THE CHIEF

In Hawaiian evolutionary theory, humans stood at the top of evolved nature. At the pinnacle of human society, and therefore of all else, stood the *ali'i nui* (high chief or king). The *ali'i nui* was thought to have a special relationship with nature, a nurturing and sustaining control.

The high chiefs sometimes demonstrated their power over nature in dramatic ways, such as by halting lava flows. King Kamehameha I is said to have saved his fishponds from approaching lava by standing before the flow, making offerings, and appeasing the goddess Pele, who indwelt the flowing lava.

Newspaper accounts and letters of missionaries tell of a similar event witnessed in 1881 when Princess Ruth, who rejected the Christian religion of the *haole* (white person), demonstrated the power of both her station and of the old religion by standing before a lava flow at the outskirts of Hilo, making offerings to that presence of Pele, and stopping the flow.

The Hawaiian word *ea* means "the living breath." Even more specifically, it is the "life-force" which manifests itself as breath in people, and which also exists in everything in the cosmos. For most ancient peoples, the living breath was the sign that the life-force dwelt in a person. When one stopped breathing, the life-force had gone.

The chief's relation with the lands was so intertwined that when he died, the lands also died. The chant "Fallen is the Chief" relates this. At the death of Chief Keoua, the chant says:

> Puna is dead! Puna is dead!
> **The breath of life** (*ea*) and the breathing are gone.
> The spirit has fled.

The soul of the land, and "its living breath" (*ke ea o ka 'aina*), left it just as the chief's soul and his living breath (*ea*) left his body.

The presence of the living chief held everything together: the gods, humans, and nature. When the chief died, everything came apart: people's relationship with the lands, people's relationship with the gods, and people's relationship with others – the whole societal structure. People went about nude and engaged in sexual acts in public. They gashed themselves, knocked out their teeth, shaved their heads, and burned marks on their bodies to remember the chief. The *kapu* system (the religious laws or taboos) also fell apart, completing the disorder throughout all of nature: women entered the *heiau*, ate bananas, coconuts, and pork, and climbed over the sacred places. And women and men ate together – all acts punishable by death under the *kapu* system.

It then devolved upon the new *ali'i nui* to renew life to the land and to restore order to nature. After the mourning period, when the new *ali'i nui* was enthroned, the direction and structure of society were restored, reestablishing order among the people by reinstating the *kapu* system. Through presence and prayers, the chief then built a new relationship with the gods and with nature, revivifying nature and setting everything right again. The chant "Fallen is the Chief" tells of a new chief as he takes over the land.

> The island was untamed, that the chief knew well.
> On his becoming guardian it was more and more tamed.
> He fed the small fish,
>   he gathered them together like bonito.
> Streams of country people of the island follow;
> Now the tail of the land wags
> Like that of a well-fed favorite dog.

Once the new chief reestablished the *kapu* system and restored order to society, and once he calmed nature and brought it under his nurturing control, then it once more could be said *Ua mau ke ea o ka 'aina* (The living breath of the land continues on) *i ka pono* (since [the king is in his place of leadership and] everything is ordered correctly again).

This whole belief system is exemplified in a situation that arose in 1843 in which King Kamehameha III was temporarily forced to cede rule of the islands to Britain. He knew when he ceded that his action would cause a rupture in his chiefly, nurturing rapport with the lands. The lands themselves would suffer during this time of cession. But he had hopes that once the lands were returned he could again bring them under his chiefly nurturing power, and they would flourish as they had.

After 5 months of British occupation, on July 31, 1843, the lands were restored to the king by Admiral Thomas. At that time King

Kamehameha III came before the people again on the steps of Kawaiahaʻo Church and proclaimed, *Ua mau ke ea o ka ʻaina i ka pono* (The lands breathe again, nature lives on and prospers, now that the king has been restored to his proper place and has resumed his nurturing relationship with it – now that things are properly ordered again).

THE HAWAIIAN EXPERIENCE OF REALITY

The chants of the Hawaiians told them that they had descended from the cosmos itself and from its many plant and animal species. They felt a kinship with nature not experienced by people who see a break between humankind and the species of nature which have preceded them in the evolutionary advance. In the Western world, where the cleavage is most pronounced, animals are disdained as having senses but no reason; the plant world is recognized as alive, but in no way even aware; and the elements of the cosmos are treated as inert objects that follow mechanical laws. Hawaiians, on the other hand, view all these beings as sentient ancestral forms that interrelate with them as family. Therefore, they experience reality differently because of these views.

The difference in how the Hawaiian and the Westerner experience reality can be illustrated by the reaction of a person in an unfamiliar building who, rushing to a meeting late, opens one door and finds a storeroom filled with canned items, then opens another which is the front door to a lecture in session. Entering the "empty" storeroom elicits a totally different response than entering a lecture room full of people, even though one might not know a single person in the disturbed lecture. Canned items on shelves mean nothing to a person; they lack that which gives them significance: consciousness. The storeroom is "empty." The people in the lecture give meaning to the other encounter. It is their consciousness, their seeing a person blunder which makes the difference. The surprise and embarrassment the person experiences come about because of the people's consciousness, and with it their ability to relate and to help or hurt. These are all perceived immediately and undifferentiated from the appearance of their bodies in a person's total comprehension of the scene. Recognized consciousness makes demands on the perceiver, demands for correct behavior and correct relationship. For the Hawaiians, there are no empty storerooms. Confronting the world about them, they experience conscious beings at every turn, and along with this their interpersonal demands.

Further, there is also a real difference between coming upon someone recognized as a relative and meeting someone who is not. In perceiving one who is kin, a person experiences not only an added awareness of relationship, but also an emotional feeling of belongingness.

As Hawaiians view the world, what they actually *see* is the same as what Westerners see, but what they *perceive as seen* is different. It might be noted that Hawaiians of the past and many Hawaiians today are unaware that others do – or even can – perceive things without perceiving them as conscious and related to them as kin.

It is true that most Hawaiians today do not formally learn the traditional philosophy as it is described in these pages. Yet they approach the world in a Hawaiian way that fits hand-in-glove with the philosophy. Hawaiian philosophy mirrors a centuries-old approach to life which cannot be expunged from the culture. The Hawaiians who ache for the land as they watch Westerners – and now the Asians – buy it up and pave it over may not be able to say *how* they are related to the land, but they know they are in their bones. The Hawaiians who put their lives on the line standing in front of a bulldozer may not know why they must defend the land in that way, but they cannot turn away. With or without the philosophical tradition, Hawaiians know that they form a community with nature around them. Nature constantly and consciously in good faith provides for and protects them, and they are compelled from deep within to protect nature in turn. They do this with the same courage and bravery non-Hawaiians summon to defend *their* family and community from an aggressor.

Special Overview

THE ROLE OF ETHICS, CULTURE, AND RELIGION IN CONSERVING BIODIVERSITY: A BLUEPRINT FOR RESEARCH AND ACTION

J. Ronald Engel

I. INTRODUCTION

This paper is an exercise in practical reason – reason in the service of knowing and doing the good. It seeks to address the question, how might we make the study and practice of moral, cultural, and religious values more effective factors in preserving and restoring the earth's rapidly vanishing biodiversity? To this end, how might educators, artists, religious leaders, and scholars in the humanities and social sciences collaborate with environmental professionals and natural scientists to create a program of research and action on biodiversity ethics and values? What assumptions should guide their work? What should be the thematic focus of their enterprise? What kinds of research and action should they undertake?

Biodiversity is of such importance to the viability of human existence and the future of life on this planet, the changes required to address it so vast, the time to make them so short, and the role of values so obviously a necessary factor in any lasting solution that this question should be on the lips of many persons today. Unfortunately, given the divisions that dominate our contemporary social order and the organization of human knowledge – divisions between facts and values; the sacred and the secular; theory and practice; technical, ethical, and political modes of discourse – it is a question that is unlikely to be asked by more than a few.

Donald A. Brown (1990) accurately describes the current state of affairs as one in which environmental scientists and environmental lawyers "seem to be, at best, only dimly aware of the vast body of literature that has developed in the field of environmental ethics in the last twenty years." Consequently, he says, "environmental professionals rarely integrate environmental ethical discourse into discussions about environmental problem solving." It must be added that few persons working in the humanities or social sciences integrate environmental science and policy considerations into their discussions of norms and values, either. On what basis, then, would anyone seriously entertain the possibility of a multidisciplinary research and action program organized around the role of values in conserving biodiversity, especially a multidisciplinary program that cuts across the many cultures, faiths, and ecosystems of the world and is committed to positive social change?

Two circumstances lead me to think that the question of how to make values effective in conserving biodiversity is worth asking.

The first circumstance is contextual: there is a growing recognition in the world-at-large of the *need* to include ethics and values in environmental science and conservation practice (Engel and Engel 1990). A thumbnail summary of this trend includes passage in 1982 by the United Nations General Assembly of the *World Charter of Nature*; the first major interfaith conference on the environment held in Assisi, Italy, in 1988; the emergence of a number of national and international networks to link values and the environment, including the World Wide Fund for Nature (WWF) Network in Conservation and Religion, and the International Society for Environmental Ethics; the launching of *Caring for the Earth: A Strategy for Sustainable Living*, a blueprint for global environmental action based on the principles of a "world ethic for living sustainably," by the United Nations Environment Program (UNEP), WWF, and the World Conservation Union (IUCN) in 1991; the adoption of a code of environmental ethics and practice by the European Economic Summit Nations (Berry 1990); and the *Earth Charter* adopted by the United Nations Conference on Environment and Development in 1992. Supporting these events is a growing scholarly literature documenting the decisive impact of world view, cultural norms, and psychological attitudes and perceptions on the human treatment of nature. Although it is possible to exaggerate the role of ideas, values, and beliefs in human history, the best minds working in the field recognize the dialectical interplay between social consciousness, social structure, and physical context.

The second circumstance is the specific occasion for this paper. As chair of the IUCN Ethics, Culture, and Conservation Working Group, a volunteer network charged with the task of advising the Director General and membership of IUCN on how to most effectively promote conservation ethics, I was invited in June 1990 to prepare a proposal that addressed the ethical, cultural, and spiritual dimensions of the international Biodiversity Strategy Programme, organized by the World Resources Institute (WRI), IUCN, and UNEP, and involving more than forty governmental and nongovernmental organizations around the world. The program objectives were to develop factual information about biodiversity, to build a broad-based movement to seek improved policies and expanded action to conserve biodiversity, and to provide technical advice on biodiversity conservation. The first product of the program, the *Global Biodiversity Strategy* (WRI, IUCN, and UNEP 1992), provides guidelines for action to save, study, and sustainably and equitably use Earth's biodiversity.

In the summer of 1990 I sent an invitation to selected members of the IUCN ethics network and other experts, soliciting their participation and suggestions. The response was overwhelming. During the next year, eighty persons from twenty-three countries provided thoughtful, often extensive input, which became the basis for this paper. (Unless otherwise noted, quotations are taken directly from this correspondence.) Earlier drafts were presented and discussed at the

XVIII General Assembly of IUCN and the XVII Pacific Science Congress. The *Global Biodiversity Strategy* includes a summary of this proposal and the recommendation that it be funded at a level adequate for a decade of serious work.

What follows must be regarded as preliminary, tentative, and visionary, and this for three reasons. First, as Adil Najam notes, "It would require a major international polling of ideas, experiences, and views to develop the ethical, cultural, and spiritual dimensions of a truly global biodiversity strategy." Neither the time nor the resources were available to do this, and neither will be until a program similar to the one envisaged here is undertaken. If such were available, a greater level of participation from countries outside the United States and from women could have been achieved.

Second, obviously only a major university or research center would have the leadership capacity in initiating a program of the breadth and depth outlined here. Indeed, the proposed model of institutional organization in Part IV involves a network of major research centers throughout the world. Consequently, this proposal may be considered much too ambitious for the resources likely to be available. However, the *Global Biodiversity Strategy*, which was launched in 1992 by WRI, IUCN, and UNEP (in association with other United Nations agencies and cooperating organizations), calls for a program of *scientific and technical research and management* of much greater magnitude, with funding in the billions of dollars. If the role of values in the conservation of biodiversity is of the importance that many of the most informed scientists and public and academic leaders believe it to be, then the proposal that follows, far from being overambitious, is one of the most reasonable and realistic calls for research and action that could be conceived under the circumstances (Wilson 1988). At the very least, it offers a comprehensive framework that may help to orient and inspire more discrete and manageable projects.

Third, since the consultants have not been able to meet as a group, this representation of their ideas and interests is subject to my own limitations. Wherever feasible, I have included actual comments from the papers I received. I believe that a consensus prevails regarding Part II, Basic Assumptions, and most of the specific suggestions contributed appear in Parts III and IV, the Project Theme and the Project Proposal, respectively.

The terms "biodiversity," "ethics," "culture," and "religion" are defined as used in this overview.

"Biodiversity" is typically used to identify the "variety and variability of the organisms that inhabit a specified place, be it a pond, coral reef, forest, continent or planet" (Beattie 1991). The *Global Biodiversity Strategy* expands this meaning to embrace the variety of genes, species, habitats, ecosystems, and human cultures that compose the biosphere (Reid and Miller 1989).

"Ethics" refers to both the actual moral judgments and actions that people make regarding what they consider to be personally and socially virtuous, right or good, and to the moral reasoning they use to justify such judgments and actions.

"Culture" is used in the broad sense, inclusive of both the "high culture" and "ethos" of a people, and of all human value-bearing activities, social, economic, and political, but with special emphasis on the pursuits of art, knowledge, and religion.

"Religion" or "spirituality" refers to the ultimate frame of reference (myth, world view, belief system), simultaneously evaluative and factual (or ontological), in terms of which cultural ideals are formed and ethical decisions made. It does not necessarily convey a belief in a supreme or divine being.

II. BASIC ASSUMPTIONS

1. Biodiversity is a fact and a value.

Biodiversity exists in the world as an objective reality, a value-laden fact of nature, independent of human valuing and knowing. But what biodiversity means to human beings, and whether and how we maintain, enhance, or deplete it, is a matter of our perceptions of this reality, and of our interactions with it, and hence a matter of human knowledge and values. There is no way of talking about biodiversity, scientific or otherwise, or of acting on its behalf, that does not involve human interpretation. In a world dominated by human action, the fate of biodiversity will be determined by what we know about it, and how we choose to value it.

Maria Luisa Cohen raises the reality of biodiversity as both fact and value when she writes: "It is evident that what has been extolled as the 'beauty of nature,' its sensual appeal, is nothing else than the realization of what ecologists call biodiversity." She echoes Umberto Eco's (1983) insight that the "beauty of the cosmos derives not only from unity in variety but from variety in unity."

Francesco Escobar: "I find it important to review the conceptualization at the basis of biodiversity conservation, because if the idea is that the main causal factors are strictly biological, ecological, geographic or geological, there is only a very secondary role for the arts, the philosopher, the humanist, and the social scientist. It is important to reveal the multiple components of the environmental problem; the non-social aspects are real and demand to be properly addressed, but the social ones are paramount and require urgent and difficult response."

It follows that values and moral choices are present in every aspect of action on behalf of biodiversity. To juxtapose economic and other "tangible" or "utilitarian" approaches with those that stress so-called "intangible" moral and spiritual values is misleading. All human relationships to the environment are tangible and value-laden. The real contrast is between different *kinds* of tangible relationships and their associated values, and the crucial question is how to create an ethical framework that makes the most fundamental relationships – economic productivity, ecological sustainability, social justice, aesthetic enjoyment – mutually supportive. Success in conserving biodiversity will depend on success in understanding how different cultural factors affect the destruction and preservation of biodiversity, how cultural change occurs, and how the sort of cultural change that promotes biodiversity can be encouraged.

2. Biological diversity and cultural diversity depend on one another, and in many cases must be preserved together.

Biodiversity is a multivocal term. It means different things to different people in different cultures. Cultural differences may enrich (or in some cases diminish) our appreciation for the meaning of biological diversity; conversely, biological diversity is a primary source of the world's rich cultural diversity. In many places throughout the world, the loss of healthy social, cultural, and economic diversity is part of the same process as the loss of biological diversity. A strategy for protecting and restoring biodiversity must be rooted in a strong affirmation of *the value of diversity as such*, including the diverse ways in which diverse cultures utilize and maintain the diversity of life.

Baird Callicott: "Diverse conservation values and ethics – differently grounded and articulated, but pragmatically convergent – should be developed out of indigenous worldviews and asserted as a matter of local autonomy and pride."

A special problem is posed by the role of distinctly "Western" or "liberal individualist and rationalist" values in creating the biodiversity crisis and in its solution. While the contemporary problem is no doubt precipitated by certain types of Western values and institutions, by the same token, any answer will have to be operational in Western societies and therefore use at least some fundamental Western categories.

3. The challenge of the next decade is for persons in every society to find and create ethics of biodiversity adequate to the twenty-first century.

In the past, the knowledge and values that maintained and enhanced biodiversity were often woven into the cultural wisdom and inherited practices of the people. Today, no culture manifests an ethic of biodiversity adequate to the social and technological conditions of modern life. In fact, the dominant norms of so-called "modern" and "developed" cultures are primary factors responsible for the destruction of biodiversity.

The moral challenge is unprecedented: against the threat of massive extinctions, to maintain the biological foundations for human existence and for the continuing evolution of life on earth. Never before have human societies had the power and duty to plan for biodiversity and never before have we had to act on a planetary scale. Never before have human societies faced the need to undertake deliberately the rapid transformation of their own most fundamental world views. No less than a new development vision for world history, one that "nourishes and perpetuates the historical fulfillment of the whole community of life on Earth," is required (Engel and Engel 1990).

Jean Matthews: "Never before in the history of the planet has a life form had to face its own role in its environment, weigh its responsibilities as a species, consider the long-range effects of its action on its environment and itself, and then try to modify its behavior and measure the results of its modifications ... scientifically, economically, psychologically, and ethically. Can we really, as 'never before,' consciously and deliberately define an ethic and then *build* an ethical society?"

However, if values are to be effective in individual and social life, and if they are to be truly *ethical* values, they must be the creative work of the people themselves as they exercise their moral freedom and conscience. Moral values, by definition, are self-chosen. Although it is possible to *help lead* this process, no person or institution can make it happen.

Truly viable ethics of biodiversity will come out of the creative struggles of persons in every society to:

- face the reality of what is happening and why

- appreciate their own involvement and responsibility

- acknowledge personal and collective moral failure and ignorance

- find guidance in the teachings of the most relevant cultural and religious traditions

- grasp the implications of the modern evolutionary and ecological world view

- listen to the voice of conscience and to redemptive meanings beyond the forms of human speech

- learn from what others are doing in other parts of the world

- cultivate with the help of poetry, art, drama, and ritual a perception of the world as a wondrous reality

- engage with fellow citizens in reasoned moral dialogue, decision, and action to safeguard and extend biodiversity

4. The ethical challenge of global biodiversity is one with the ethical challenge of how to build an economically, politically, and socially just and secure world.

The fate of biodiversity cannot be separated from fundamental social choices and power conflicts. The issue of biodiversity is inextricably intertwined with issues of racism, social and economic injustice, lack of education and health care, and the inequitable relationships between nations; the conservation of biodiversity requires the consent and participation of those who are the victims of economic and social injustice. If significant biodiversity is to survive into the next century, it must be at the *center* of the social agenda, not at the periphery.

Len Webb: "One thing that strikes me again and again is the 'reductionist' flavour of separating 'biodiversity' (as an abstraction) from species-rich ecosystems; and of conceiving biodiversity as somehow *not* enmeshed in politics and economics, avarice and ignorance. ... We should not continue to deceive ourselves by euphemisms. ... The 'root causes' of biodiversity loss are not legislative/administrative but economic/political."

Contributors to this paper raised one or more of the particular social issues that are intertwined with biodiversity, and yet often omitted from its study and conservation:

- interrelations among biodiversity, population pressure, poverty and the power relations between North and South (Richard Tucker)

- the necessity for a new ethics of family planning and consumption (Daniel Janzen)

- issues of war and national security (Len Ackland and Arthur Westing)

- patterns of production and consumption, trade systems, transportation systems, housing patterns, legal structures including meanings of property (Douglas Sturm)

- abolition of all forms of religious, ethnic, racial, class, and national prejudice (William Gregg)

Many contributors conceive these issues as interrelated parts of one contemporary global problematique – the "modern development process," with its drive to dominate nature and people through reductionist science, perpetual economic growth, cultural uniformity, mechanized mass production and consumption, and concentration of wealth and power.

Denis Goulet: "No ethic of biodiversity is possible without a revolution in (this) development model. Only a paradigm of 'authentic development,' of which sustainability is only one note, can be compatible with biodiversity."

Inevitably, there are tensions between the values of biodiversity and values associated with the quest for justice and security. One of the major tasks of work in biodiversity ethics is to address these conflicts, and develop norms and procedures by which they may be adjudicated to pioneer a new concept of ethics – environmental social ethics.

5. Profound transformations in religious attitudes and institutions are required if biodiversity is to be preserved.

Contemporary threats to biodiversity are of such an order of magnitude that it is difficult to conceive how more and better management, knowledge, education, political participation, or economic incentives will suffice. The grip of the modern development world view is so strong that only a fundamental shift in what people believe to be of ultimate concern will be powerful enough to motivate them to search for a more ethical relationship to the diversity of life, and effect the change in heart and in social behavior required.

Historically, religious myth, symbol, and ritual have served as the primary vehicles for defining good and evil, and for motivating personal and collective transformation. Also, religions and their associated philosophical systems are a primary way whereby human beings seek to address the problem of the one and the many – and hence the fact of "diversity" and "plurality" in existence.

But the power of the great religious faiths, ancient and modern, has so far been inadequate to achieve a just and peaceful world. Most religious teachings and institutions require considerable transformation if they are to incorporate contemporary scientific knowledge and cooperate with each other in addressing the basic biological and human needs of the planet. Yet there is strong evidence that religious communities throughout the world are beginning to respond positively to the global environmental crisis and to challenge the great dualisms of spirit and nature, sacred and secular, that have compromised their own most authentic and liberating teachings. In addition, much can be learned from contemporary movements for a new "spirituality of the Earth" based on holistic understandings of the ecology of humanity and nature.

However difficult the problems involved, an initiative that seriously proposes to reverse the decline in the world's biodiversity cannot avoid the religious question. If it is to win commitment sufficient to accomplish its purposes, it must be conceived as serving a vision of life larger than survival and material well-being.

6. A basic problem is to achieve a healthy relationship between theory and practice.

A *praxis* is needed for addressing the issues of biodiversity: to integrate theory and practice, the abstract and the concrete, the verbal and nonverbal, ethics as reflection and ethics as action. To retain the theory/practice split is to maintain the entrenched power relationships that are destroying the environment.

Cliff Cobb: "On an abstract level, almost everyone favors the concept of biodiversity. Thus there is a danger that an ethics based on this abstract concept will never rise above the level of banality or truism. Indeed, such ethics can serve as a cloak for the continuation of business as usual and divert attention from controversial policy choices."

William Simpson: "Contemporary environmental discussion must rely on scientific categories, language, and procedural logic. These are notoriously abstract and unpersuasive in public life. They are easily countered by rhetorically facile and swift interpretations, and the constant, repetitive, programmed graphics of consumer demand stimulation."

One attack upon the theory/practice split is to map the empirical connections between symbolic actions and behavioral changes.

Stephen Sterling: "A basic problem is to advance a systemic understanding of links between action and effect, particularly when the links are often separated by time and space."

Another line of attack is to promote direct experience of the natural environment, including the aesthetic experience of nature mediated by the arts, stories, drama, myth, ritual, in such a way as to ground and supplement merely verbal and theoretical discussions of values and ethics.

Arne Naess: "Moralizing has its important place but is fairly ineffective. ... People should be introduced to situations which elicit care of nature as a natural inclination."

Maria Luisa Cohen: "We are still waiting for the artists and writers who will transform the new scientific knowledge and the moral concern about the environment into new structures of expression which will deliver to us what this new knowledge and sentiment means for the loves and attachments, sorrows and joys, horrors and delights, of any human existence."

On the one hand, the theoretical tools of ethics can provide powerful analytic and evaluative means for investigating the structure of human interactions with other humans and with the Earth. On the other hand, these theoretical tools need to be rooted in actual practices and experiences and applied to concrete social situations if they are to empower persons to effect social change. It follows that any serious attempt to promote the influence of ethics, culture, and religion in the conservation of biodiversity must occur in partnership with existing action programs that are seeking to nurture an affective appreciation of nature and influence a specific set of social obligations in a specific ecological context.

7. Work on the ethics and values of biodiversity should be guided by multilateral approaches.

Multilateral thinking emphasizes the multiplicity of factors that interact to determine any significant ecological or social outcome. To adopt a multilateral approach means:

- combining a variety of morally inspired actions in any strategy to conserve biodiversity (e.g., religious transformation, publicly accessible scientific knowledge, artistic expression, personal moral reflection and choice, local community empowerment, governmental action, changes in the global market system, and legal agreements)

- working with communities that are both geographically and authoritatively inclusive and overlapping (e.g., simultaneously attending to local, national, and international institutions and values)

- pursuing intersectorial cooperation and decision making; iden-

tifying the different kinds of human institutions and activities
that have a stake in any particular ecosystem

* developing cross-disciplinary approaches, with participation
  from the natural sciences, social sciences, the arts and humanities

*8. Promoting the ethics of biodiversity is part of the task of build-
ing a new world ethic.*

Although it is not necessary or desirable that the world have a uniform
religion or ideology, it does need some binding norms, values, ideals,
and goals. Some of the most important of the norms and principles
needed to govern the world's cultural diversity are articulated in the
Universal Declaration of Human Rights. Work on behalf of the ethics
of biodiversity must be conceived as part of the effort to expand our
understanding of a "world ethic" to include the ethics of our treatment
of the Earth's biotic diversity.

The process of building a global consensus on fundamental
ethical principles of biological diversity is already well underway.
The World Charter for Nature (Burhenne and Irwin 1983) affirms that
"Every form of life is unique, warranting respect regardless of its
worth to man, and, to accord other organisms such recognition, man
must be guided by a moral code of action." *Caring for the Earth* – the
new World Conservation Strategy – affirms the following among the
elements of a "world ethic for living sustainably": "Every life form
warrants respect and preservation independently of its worth to
people. People should ensure the survival of all species, and safeguard
their habitats. They should treat all creatures decently, and protect
them from cruelty, avoidable suffering, and unnecessary killing."

It follows that whatever is done to develop the ethical, cultural,
and religious dimensions of biodiversity, conservation should build
upon these existing documents.

9. The bioregion is an especially important locus for work in
biodiversity ethics and values.

The history of human ecology teaches us that, until the modern era, each distinct geographical region was a more or less integrated and self-sufficient *biogeocultural community*, sustained by a variety of reciprocal relationships between land, air, water, and the diversity of human and nonhuman organisms. An especially vivid example of the integration of culture and landscape exists in Australian Aboriginal societies (see Chapter 5 in this book). It is difficult to conceive how biodiversity can be preserved, much less restored, apart from through reconstitution of the biosphere as a community of such communities.

The social forces that destroy biological diversity are the same social forces that disrupt and disperse the human communities whose lives are determined by particular habitats and regions. If these forces are to be transformed, changes must occur *within* each region, as well as in the relationships that bind the many regions together. However, the power necessary to make these changes is not only local, but national and international.

Ethics conducive to the preservation of biodiversity are often grounded in the unique ecological and cultural history and resources of the local region and its special "sense of place" (Norton 1991). The bioregional myths, stories, and sacred places that symbolize the beauty and drama of a particular landscape often provide deep insights into the region's most important biological values and the motivation for their preservation. The great world religions derive much of their poetry and universal appeal from their association with a particular landscape conceived as a parable of universal truths.

The locus for the most effective action on behalf of biodiversity is frequently among the people who are most intimately acquainted with a region, both those who wrest their livelihood from it and those who take a special interest in its history, integrity, and future.

David Given: "The need is to meet people on their ground and in their fora where they are comfortable and where they can feel at home and free to participate ... here is also where we can involve the innovative, younger, poorer people who are close to the workface of conservation."

William Simpson: "The identification of the bioregion as a primary locus of research and action establishes an ethical principle – the point from which thought and action proceed toward particular understanding and change. And it is a multiple principle, a plural ethic: diverse understandings, coherences, claims, communities, and achievements must be won, all relative to different bioregions of evolutionary time and space. So the biodiverse Good is not everywhere and always the same. Particularity qualifies the universal more obviously than universal categories include regional variation and innovation."

A major practical and theoretical challenge is to reconcile the tension between the particular ethics of diverse biogeocultural areas and the need for a common world ethic by which to enable the mutual flourishing of all regions.

10. The role of ethics, culture, and religion needs to be attended to with the same seriousness and institutional and financial support as any other aspect of work on behalf of the conservation of biodiversity.

Biodiversity conservation will be only as intelligent as the knowledge base on which it is built. Knowledge about how ethics, culture, and religion affect human behavior is an essential component in mapping any effective strategy for the conservation of biodiversity. It follows that persons with expert knowledge in these fields need to be included as full team members of biodiversity conservation programs throughout the world.

If we are serious about motivating the world to restore the full glory of life on Earth, we must overcome the gap separating the technical-scientific world knowledge regime (environmental scientists, natural resource managers, policy specialists, and development experts) from the creators and transmitters of cultural symbols, values, and myths (artists, writers, educators, humanists, social scientists, religious and moral leaders).

III. PROJECT THEME: PROMOTING ECOLOGICAL CITIZENSHIP

Research and action in ethics and values require a unifying theme if it is to be conceptually coherent and practically effective. One promising theme is "citizenship," specifically the synthesis of democratic citizenship and ecological citizenship. This theme has been implicit at several points in the previous section; it is time now to make it explicit.

The quest for democratic citizenship is one of the most potent political, economic, and social forces at work in the world today. The drive toward greater respect for the rights of the individual, for shared participation in the decisions and responsibilities of public life, for equity in the distribution of resources and opportunities, and for the right of self-determination by local communities is evident in diverse societies. Many of the new citizen initiatives are being undertaken on behalf of environmental as well as political and economic purposes (Havel 1986). Given the deep reciprocal connections between poverty and environmental degradation, it is reasonable to say that conservation of biodiversity will only succeed if it makes positive linkages to the world-wide democratic revolution – and the world-wide democratic revolution will only succeed if it issues in a strong ecological, as well as political, understanding of citizenship.

Responsible citizenship is a foundational principle of the *Global Biodiversity Strategy*. The strategy affirms that "it is local communities who hold the ultimate responsibility for conserving biodiversity, and the ultimate right to seek their livelihoods from it." Kenton Miller notes that the roots of poverty and loss of biodiversity, North and South, are in the "overall lack of involvement of people in the planning and management of their environments and futures" (McNeely et al. 1990). Vandana Shiva, in her critique of early drafts of the *Global Biodiversity Strategy*, argues that it should be renamed a "people's biodiversity plan" in order to make clear that the people, especially the people of tropical countries, own the world's biodiversity, that they are the ones who are responsible for its maintenance and the ones who should benefit from its exploitation. Many persons have noted that biodiversity conservation cannot succeed if it is perceived to be the job of government, business corporations, or public interest organizations, and not the job of the people themselves.

Citizenship is a comprehensive moral ideal. It means co-equality with others in responsibility for the good of the community as a whole, and participation in the benefits of the life of the community as a whole. In most societies it involves concepts of rights as well as of duties. It requires a sense of basic respect for the worth of persons different from ourselves. Therefore, citizenship is one of the most powerful concepts by which persons have sought to define the appropriate place of humans in the natural order. We frequently speak today of the ideal of "planetary citizenship." Aldo Leopold (1949) called for a new "land ethic" that would "change the role of *Homo sapiens* from conqueror of the land-community to plain member and citizen of it." If the concept of the "rights of nature" or "respect for nature" has any meaning, it is by virtue of this enlargement of the meaning of citizenship to include our place in the natural created order.

Citizenship conceived as a moral as well as political category encourages a creative cultural pluralism that can build a global civilization upon the best each society has to offer. In the East, for example, citizenship was present in the Sherpa custom of *shing-i-nawa*, or forest guards, that effectively protected the biological diversity in Bhutan for hundreds of years (McNeely 1985). This concept is also deeply rooted in Western secular and religious thought. An understanding of universal moral citizenship may be the best way to withstand the dangers of resurgent ethnic nationalisms sometimes associated with efforts to preserve particular places and ecosystems.

Citizenship is actual. Every person is either a citizen of some human community and local ecosystem or suffers the plight of a person whose citizenship is denied. The reality of citizenship links each individual to local, national, and international levels of political organization and to the constitutions and legal agreements that order them. In principle, "We the peoples of the united nations," not the governments of the many nations, wrote the *Charter of the United Nations*. Thus it is by virtue of our identity as citizens of the United Nations that we can consider the *World Charter for Nature* morally binding. Similarly, by virtue of our rights as citizens of the United Nations, we have the opportunity to jointly form international voluntary associations to work on behalf of such public values as biodiversity. The task of making the ideal of ecological citizenship actual is a task for everyone and every society in the world. Citizenship thus assures that our ethics will be concrete rather than abstract, and will relate to real life issues and choices, not theoretical debates.

Citizenship pinpoints what is at stake when we lament the failure of environmental ethics to govern human affairs. If the economic system fails to preserve biodiversity, it is because we have failed as citizens to devise the kind of economic institutions that will preserve it. If the political system fails to act on behalf of biodiversity, it is because we have failed as citizens to hold it accountable. Citizenship places moral responsibility where it belongs – in what we do or fail to do as communities of citizens. As responsible citizens, it also requires us to face the many obstacles (e.g., inequitable concentrations of wealth and power, authoritarian rule, poverty, ignorance, war).

There is reason to believe that those societies most successful in conserving biodiversity, for instance, indigenous and traditional cultures, are societies governed by a unified mythic system or civic faith that integrates evolution and revolution. What kind of civic faith is available today that can reconcile evolution and revolution? What new public myth can replace the dominant secular myth of perpetual progress through economic growth, and do so in a way that is culturally and ecologically appropriate for each biogeocultural region?

IV. Project Proposal: Research and Action in Biodiversity Ethics

In order to enhance the impact of ethics, culture, and religion on the conservation of biodiversity throughout the world, the IUCN Ethics, Culture, and Conservation Working Group proposes that a consortium of private and public funding agencies establish a Biodiversity Ethics Project. This project has three primary aims:

1. to establish a Global Biodiversity Ethics Network, a collaborative effort of institutions and individuals concerned for research and action on the role of ethics, culture, and religion in conserving biodiversity;

2. to strengthen the capacity of national and international organizations to promote biodiversity ethics; and

3. to strengthen the leadership capacity of individuals and groups in developing effective biodiversity ethics in local bioregions.

It is assumed that the actual embodiment and practice of democratic and ecological citizenship in local communities is both the beginning and end of the project, and that each of these three aims seeks to effect this goal. The proposals that follow are representative rather than definitive or exhaustive.

1. Building a Global Biodiversity Ethics Network

Founding the network. Expand the present list of consultants to create an international network of individuals and institutions with expert capacities in environmental and development ethics, religion, and the social sciences, and in the science and management of biodiversity, to serve as the basic organizational structure for the Biodiversity Ethics Project. The network should include institutions with field projects underway, and with strong community relations, and should connect with other major policy and research initiatives in global change research and action. It should be headquartered in a major university or research center. The early establishment of the network would assure the resources necessary for a much broader sampling of ideas, experiences, and views prior to the planning of the actual project.

Collegial development. Empower the participants in the Biodiversity Ethics Network to speak and work together on behalf of the values of biodiversity by sharing and reflecting on their personal and professional value-commitments. Ideally, this should happen in cross-cultural contexts so that underlying differences of perspectives can be appreciated. The premise here is that the participants in the network are already bearers of key biodiversity values.

Len Webb: "Why don't we begin by educating ourselves? For example, we should hold small, personal discussion groups which would deal with personal testaments about what motivates us; what is the history of our conviction, involvement, and now our ecological intuition and morality?"

Methodology for action/research. Develop a methodology for research and action, including criteria for defining a biologically and culturally healthy biogeocultural area, and for deciding what constitutes "success" in promoting the ethics of biodiversity. Other fields, such as human rights or health care, can be used as models. One promising instrument of assessment would be the use of "sustainable development indicators" (Goulet 1991). It will also be necessary to develop both the ethical criteria by which to rank the variety of values at stake in decisions involving biodiversity and a process for arbitrating value conflicts.

Biodiversity ethics symposia and publications. Hold a series of symposia to address the basic moral, cultural, and religious concepts and issues in the conservation of biodiversity. These symposia should result in a series of publications that can effectively communicate with a wide audience. Varying degrees of new research will be needed to prepare for these symposia. Their primary purpose, however, is to bring together and evaluate the work already being done by scholars throughout the world and to identify new work that needs to be done. Examples of topics to be considered include:

- *images and metaphors* of biodiversity in the world's cultures, philosophies, and religions, with special attention to examples that shed light on how such images (or their absence) currently function to define public perceptions of biodiversity, and how they might be more effectively used to motivate public concern. Examples include E. O. Wilson's idea of biodiversity as "biotic capital"; Aldo Leopold's idea that we should "keep every cog and wheel" in the land organism/mechanism; the notion that endangered species are like rare artistic masterpieces. This study needs to include a critique of such images and metaphors from the standpoint of moral, aesthetic, religious, and scientific adequacy, as well as an examination of how they hide or expose social and economic biases and interests. For example, does the use of the metaphor of biodiversity as the "common heritage of mankind" help to camouflage the inequitable utilization of biological resources (Shiva 1990)?

- *justifications for preserving biodiversity* from a variety of contemporary philosophical and theological perspectives (including utilitarian and economic), the various kinds of ethical argumentation involved, and an attempt to identify the strengths, limits, and practical contributions of each to selected policy questions. Special attention should be devoted to how claims that natural things have value in themselves may be defended and effective in action for biodiversity.

- the *key issues* of biodiversity, including the political, social, economic, cultural, and ethical dimensions of each, and the most morally adequate responses. Such issues include the treatment of domesticated and wild animals, protection of endangered species, animal patenting and biotechnology, the privatization of the biotic commons and the professional and commercial uses of traditional knowledge, economic equity in the exploitation and preservation of biotic resources within and between nations, population policy and family planning, the role of women in the maintenance of biodiversity, and the impact of the modern culture of consumerism.

- the relation of biodiversity to *human experience and fulfillment.* Andrew Brennan asks: "Is there a conception of human nature and human flourishing implicit in our approach to political and policy questions? What should it be? What is the fulfillment of human life, including the fulfillment of the species history, in evolution?"

- the *experience of native peoples* as it contributes to the ethics of biodiversity, including an evaluation of what cultural wisdom can be meaningfully transferred to modern industrial societies, and how to promote effective moral respect for the rights of indigenous peoples.

- the relation of *ethics, religion, and science,* bringing into one conversation those working on the metaphysical, religious, and scientific bases for a new ecological world view with natural resource experts and policymakers concerned about biodiversity.

- *the history of the global landscape,* how biodiversity has changed because of human intervention in the past five thousand years, and the major cultural factors involved.

- *the potential of democratic ecological citizenship,* including questions such as: Can citizenship be a vehicle for exercising environmental justice in complex modern societies, and if not, what are the alternatives? What secular and religious myths, symbols, and teachings now promote responsible citizenship in each of the major cultures of the world? Do these also involve notions of ecological citizenship? If not, how might they be reinterpreted to do so? How does "democracy" function today as a civic faith and myth of citizenship for many societies? In what ways has it been extended to include principles of ecological citizenship? What is the value or disvalue of "liberalism"? What new institutions are necessary to discharge the responsibilities of ecological citizenship?

Strategic issue development. Select a series of critical issues or conflicts involving biodiversity and develop actionable proposals for the most morally adequate response and resolution. This entails a readiness to confront injustice and unethical environmental behavior, and the willingness and capacity to intervene constructively in diverse arenas of social practice and decision making. Part of this task is the identification of the political, social, economic, and ideological coalitions that are needed to build an adequate global power base for placing biodiversity at the center of the social agenda.

2. Strengthening the capacities of national and international organizations to promote biodiversity ethics

Each of these proposals suggests ways in which the Biodiversity Ethics Network can *collaborate* with various sectors and institutional initiatives that impact local communities.

Biodiversity ethics and the Global Biodiversity Strategy. Facilitate the integration of ethical, cultural, and religious considerations into each component of the program of scientific research and management recommended by the *Global Biodiversity Strategy*. This will require collaborative work with the partners of the strategy and their associated organizations, such as the Species Survival Commission of IUCN.

Since the strategy plans to map the Earth's existing biological diversity, an example of a complementary body of work from the perspective of values might be the development of a "cultural map" of the many diverse social attitudes and practices affecting the environment.

Biodiversity and the world ethic of sustainability. Sponsor a workshop on biodiversity ethics and the proposed world ethic of "living sustainably" with representatives of the agencies responsible for implementing *Caring for the Earth*. The aim is to clarify the moral status of biodiversity (for instance, is the aim the fullest possible biodiversity, or merely the biodiversity necessary to "sustain" human life?) and how it should serve as a fundamental moral and empirical criterion for sustainable development. This must be done soon because of current proposals to define the ethics of sustainability in narrow economic and technological terms.

Biodiversity ethics and protected areas. The world's parks and protected areas now hold in trust some of the finest remnants of relatively unaltered ecosystems and therefore constitute a major resource for research and education in biodiversity. Research is needed on how these preserves can be managed for noneconomic as well as economic values, and on the kinds of cultural and religious motivations that will continue to lead to the preservation and protection of such areas.

Biodiversity ethics and nongovernmental organizations (NGOs). Participate in the development of Amnesty for Earth, as recommended in *Caring for the Earth*. Develop an action research project on how voluntary associations have emerged in modern societies as primary vehicles for ecological responsibility, their comparative cultural status and indebtedness to the Western liberal tradition, and how they may become agents for the constitution of bioregional democratic citizenship.

Biodiversity ethics and law. Create a special task force on biodiversity ethics and environmental law, for providing needed ethical expertise to the growing number of attempts by national and international bodies to draft new constitutions, environmental codes of practice, and international conventions and treaties that address environmental concerns. Examples of recent efforts to incorporate values in legal and associational agreements include the Brussels Code of the Economic Summit Nations (Berry 1990); the "Universal Code of Environmental Conduct" adopted by the NGO/Media Symposium on Communication for Environment, Bangkok, 1990; and the Global Consultation on the Development and Enforcement of International Environmental Law, with special focus on biological diversity, The Hague, September 1991. Projects in progress include the proposed International Declaration and Convention on Sustainability, the proposed International Convention on the Conservation of Biological Diversity, and the proposed Global Convention on Environmental Rights and Duties.

Douglas Sturm: "We should not focus only on national and international levels. For example, it would be productive to design and distribute model ordinances for local political arenas: villages, cities, departments, provinces, states. Having such in hand, groups of citizens would have a tool with which to lobby their local governing bodies for new legislation on biodiversity. A second focus might be preparing persons to serve as 'expert witnesses' in court cases on matters pertaining to the values of biodiversity, in analogy to the use of 'expert witnesses' on the ethics of the death penalty."

Biodiversity ethics and religion. Develop a working partnership between the Global Biodiversity Ethics Network and programs underway to create religious foundations for conservation: the program for "Justice, Peace and Integrity of Creation" of the World Council of Churches, Assisi Nature Council, the Buddhist Perception of Nature Project, UNEP Environmental Sabbath, WWF Network on Conservation and Religion.

A major opportunity for work in biodiversity ethics and religion lies in theological and ministerial education. There is a need to develop new curricula and programs for educating clerical and lay religious leaders, who are serious about the role of biodiversity in religious teaching, ritual, and practice.

Biodiversity ethics, business, and the professions. Collaborate in developing professional and commercial codes of ethics for the furtherance of biodiversity, making use of both traditional knowledge and ecological science. Collaborate with the business sector in studies on the economic, sociological, political, and moral evolution of the contemporary corporation and the possibility of its transformation into an agent for the protection and restoration of biodiversity.

Biodiversity ethics and education. Develop courses and programs in environmental ethics, with special attention to biodiversity, in schools and universities. There is a need here not only to introduce this subject into college, graduate, and professional schools, but to reform primary and secondary education to include an explicit conservation ethics component. Composition of texts for use at various levels of education is greatly needed. Uno Svedin writes: "It is mandatory to encourage attention to the ethics of biodiversity conservation within the field of biology itself!"

Make biodiversity ethics and environmental education a major field of cooperation. A number of collaborative research projects should be possible, such as a study of how and to what degree children in contemporary societies are socialized into valuing efficiency, convenience, and conformity instead of complexity and diversity. Develop and train speakers to lecture and to stimulate discussion in various settings on the values of biodiversity. Environmental education should be conceived here in the broadest sense, inclusive of the wide range of formal and informal educational experiences of which school education is only a part.

Biodiversity ethics and international fora. Work to assure adequate attention to the ethical, cultural, and religious dimensions of biodiversity in major international fora such as the IV World Congress on Protected Areas (in Venezuela 1992), and the United Nations Conference on Environment and Development (in Brazil 1992).

3. Strengthening the leadership capacity of individuals and groups in developing effective biodiversity ethics in local bioregions

Each of the following action research proposals is designed to be carried out in close collaboration with individuals and groups from one or more local bioregion, and to be directed by interdisciplinary teams from that region. Although only sketched here, these kinds of projects will increasingly become the central focus of the project as a whole and will set the agenda for work in Parts I and II. Various devices for publishing, sharing results, and coordinating resources will need to be developed.

Case studies. Develop a series of comparative case studies of biodiversity preservation incorporating ethics and values. The aim is to understand the dynamics of positive cultural change as it functions in concrete situations so that recommendations can be made for other projects. In most cases, the groups involved can help prepare the case histories and collaborate in their evaluations. Case studies should also be made of how contemporary religious traditions and organizations are affecting the preservation of biodiversity. These studies could serve as the basis for action proposals to be used in religious teaching and practice.

Integrated conservation and development pilot projects. Collaborate with integrated pilot projects that seek to transcend the sectorial approach to environmental management (e.g., the biosphere reserves and integrated regional projects of Man and the Biosphere, the Wildlands and Human Needs projects, and the African Wildlife Foundation's Protected Areas–Neighbors as Partners project). Most of these projects are directed at areas where biodiversity is especially threatened.

Defining the bioregion. Develop the concept, criteria, and methods of defining the bioregion, or "biogeocultural area," as well as how to build public understanding and awareness of the bioregion as a reality of importance to the future of biological and cultural diversity.

Urban biodiversity action research. Develop projects on the relation between urbanization and biodiversity. This is the fastest growing habitat on the planet and the site of greatest cultural diversity; yet it is usually neglected by international conservation programs, primarily because of a deep urban-humanity versus rural-nature dualism in Western thought. How urban dwellers perceive (or fail to perceive) biodiversity, how "urbanity" can be redefined to include appreciation for biodiversity as well as for cultural diversity, which perceptions of biodiversity further its restoration in urban areas, how urbanites can be mobilized on behalf of regional and global biodiversity and "sustainable cities" – these are questions that deserve serious study.

Pioneering a moral praxis in biodiversity ethics. Promote the training and representation of environmental ethicists on conservation teams. This project is modeled on the suggestive parallels between environmental ethics and bioethics – a discipline now firmly established in the field of medicine in some parts of the world.

Michael McCally: "The clinical ethicist sees to it that the principles of moral reasoning are understood and used. In practice this is often no more complex than the use of certain language: justice, fairness, autonomy, and beneficence. The important thing is that the practice takes place at the level of *particular cases and decisions*. ... A development ought to be promoted that would lead to the involvement of environmental ethicists in the 'minute particulars' of biodiversity conservation. Value issues in the biodiversity field are being dealt with all the time and decisions taken."

The belief systems of indigenous peoples. Research the role of the belief systems of indigenous peoples in maintaining biodiversity. Brendan Mackey and Judy Johnson (Centre for Resource and Environmental Studies, Australian National University) propose the following project: "Working with a team of Aboriginal people, and with biophysical and social scientists, a case study could be made asking the fundamental questions: are biodiversity ethics manifest in the Aboriginal community, and if so, how, and how can this be sustained and enhanced in the contemporary multicultural context of Australian society? Aboriginal Australians would benefit from demonstrating in an international arena the depth and relevance of their cultures to contemporary environmental problems."

Community arts. Promote the community arts – dance, music, public murals, regional writing workshops, community theater, pageantry, landscape sculpture – as a potentially powerful vehicle for introducing biodiversity ethics in local communities. Community arts typically draw upon the indigenous myths and stories of a region, often engaging the citizenry in helping to create the artistic expression itself. Local artists are likely to be receptive collaborators in local biodiversity projects.

Ethics resource libraries. Establish ethical resource libraries as parts of larger regional library collections. Most resources in biodiversity ethics (books, journals, media presentations) are too expensive for individuals in many communities of the world. These libraries might especially concentrate on resources of regional relevance and on lists of residents with special knowledge in environmental ethics.

Sacred spaces. Research the role of sacred spaces in conserving biodiversity. The sacred forests, hills, mountains, and rivers of the world hold some of the Earth's richest biodiversity and in the past were often well protected by indigenous peoples. How have sacred spaces functioned in traditional societies to bond members of communities to one another and to the land, and to protect wild species? Are similar cultural and ecological functions performed by protected areas and national parks in modern secular societies? How might such functions be enhanced?

Personal spiritual development. Explore the ways in which methods of personal spiritual guidance and self-understanding, secular and religious, may incorporate attention to the experience of biodiversity.

Citizen initiatives. Help grass-roots citizen groups to define their own ethics of biodiversity and to share their visions with other groups throughout the world. The workshop devoted to the drafting of the ethics statement for *Caring for the Earth*, at the XVII IUCN General Assembly in Costa Rica, revealed a significant interest among citizen groups such as schools and community organizations to create their own principles and codes of environmental ethics, and their creative ability to do so, once given an opportunity.

REFERENCES

Beattie, A. J. 1991. "Biodiversity and Bioresources – The Forgotten Connection." *Search* 22:59–62.
Berry, R. J. (Sam). 1990. "Environmental Knowledge, Attitudes and Action: A Code of Practice." *Science and Public Affairs* 5(2): 13–23.
Brown, Donald A. 1990. "Integrating Environmental Ethics with Science and Law." *The Environmental Professional* 12:344–350.
Burhenne, Wolfgang E., and Will A. Irwin, eds. 1983. *The World Charter for Nature*. Berlin: Erich Schmidt Verlag GmbH.
Eco, Umberto. 1983. *The Name of the Rose*. London: Secker and Warburg.
Engel, J. Ronald, and Joan Gibb Engel, eds. 1990. *Ethics of Environment and Development: Global Challenge, International Response*. Tucson: Univ. of Arizona Press.
Goulet, Denis. 1991. Development Indicators: A Research Problem, A Policy Program. Paper presented at conference for Future Research Agendas in Development, 11 July, Centre LeBret, Paris.
Havel, Vaclav. 1986. *Living in the Truth*. London: Faber and Faber.
IUCN, UNEP, and WWF. 1991. *Caring for the Earth: A Strategy for Sustainable Living*. Gland, Switzerland: IUCN.
Leopold, Aldo. 1949. *Sand County Almanac*. New York: Oxford.
McNeely, Jeffrey A. 1985. "Man and Nature in the Himalaya: What Can Be Done to Ensure That Both Can Prosper," in J. A. McNeely, J. Thorsell, and S. R. Chalise, eds., *People and Protected Areas in the Hindu-Kush Himalaya*. Kathmandu: King Mahendra Trust and ICIMOD.
McNeely, Jeffrey A., Kenton R. Miller, W. V. Reid, R. A. Mittermeier, and T. B. Werner. 1990. *Conserving the World's Biological Diversity*. IUCN, Gland, Switzerland; WRI, CI, WWF-US, and the World Bank, Washington, DC.

Norton, Bryan. 1991. *The Unity of Environmentalism.* London: Oxford University Press.

Reid, Walter V., and Kenton R. Miller. 1989. *Keeping Options Alive: The Scientific Basis for Conserving Biodiversity.* Washington, DC: World Resources Institute.

Shiva, Vandana. 1990. "Biodiversity, Biotechnology and Profit: The Need for a People's Plan to Protect Biological Diversity." *The Ecologist* 20:44–47.

Wilson, E. O., ed. 1988. *Biodiversity.* Washington, DC: National Academy Press.

WRI, IUCN, and UNEP. 1992. *Global Biodiversity Strategy: Guidelines for Action to Save, Study, and Use Earth's Biotic Wealth Sustainably and Equitably.* Washington, DC: World Resources Institute.

CONTRIBUTORS

Herson Anson is a graduate of Bulolo Forestry College, Papua New Guinea. Since then, he has been chief of the Pohnpei State Division of Forestry. He is currently the secretary to the Pohnpei State Tourist Commission and also is chair of the Pohnpei State Watershed Steering Committee.

Michael Kioni Dudley received his doctorate in Philosophy from the University of Hawai'i in1986. His dissertation, *A Philosophical Analysis of Pre-European Contact Hawaiian Thought,* was the first in-depth presentation of traditional native Hawaiian environmental philosophy and was the outgrowth of many years of studying and teaching Hawaiian religion, philosophy, and environmental thought. He teaches at Chaminade University in Hawai'i.

J. Ronald Engel, Ph.D., is Professor of Social Ethics at Meadville/ Lombard Theological School and Lecturer in Ethics and Society, Divinity School, University of Chicago. He serves as chair of the Ethics, Culture, and Conservation Working Group of the World Conservation Union, is a member of the executive committee of the International Development Ethics Association, and is on a number of other boards, including the Editorial Board of the American Journal of Theology and Philosophy, and the Advisory Board of Beacon Press. He is currently doing research for the Lilly Endowment on the spirit/nature split in Western liberal thought.

Denis Goulet is O'Neill Professor in Education for Justice at the University of Notre Dame (1979–present). He holds concurrent appointments in the Department of Economics, the Kellogg Institute for International Studies, and the Institute for International Peace Studies. After serving as research fellow at the Center for the Study of Development and Social Change in Cambridge, Massachusetts

(1970–74), Goulet became an Overseas Development Council visiting fellow (1974–76) and senior fellow (1976–79). He has worked in France, Spain, Canada, Algeria, Lebanon, Poland, Brazil, Mexico, Guinea-Bissau, and Sri Lanka, and has been a visiting professor at six institutions in five countries. He holds a doctorate in Political Science from the University of Sao Paulo, Brazil (1963).

Lawrence S. Hamilton received his Ph.D. from the University of Michigan in Natural Resources. He is a research associate at the East-West Center in Honolulu and Emeritus Professor of Forestry (Cornell University). Born and mostly educated in Canada, he served as a Zone Forester for the Ontario Department of Lands and Forests before shifting to a 29-year career in teaching and research at Cornell University. He has three times been a visiting professor in universities in Australia and New Zealand. He now works throughout Asia and the Pacific as coordinator of a Renewable Resources Program, in the Program on Environment, dealing principally with biological diversity conservation in mountains and islands.

Sonia P. Juvik, a native of Jamaica, has studied geography at McGill University, Canada; the University of Hawai'i; and the Research School of Pacific Studies, Australian National University, where she received her Ph.D. in 1982. Professor Juvik has been at the University of Hawai'i at Hilo since 1982 where she teaches in the Department of Geography and Planning. She has worked in several Pacific Islands but has concentrated most of her research in the Solomon Islands.

Poranee Natadecha-Sponsel received her early academic work in her native Thailand and went on to the USA to take work in philosophy. She received an Ed.D. (1991) in Educational Foundations from the University of Hawai'i. She is an assistant professor in the Women's Studies Program at the University of Hawai'i where she teaches an introductory course and a seminar on ecofeminism. She has taught philosophy at Kasetsart University and has conducted field studies in cultural ecology of adjacent Muslim and Buddhist villages in Thailand.

William C. Raynor received his M.Sc. from the University of Hawai'i as an East-West Center student grantee. An agroforester by training, he works for The Nature Conservancy and the U.S. Forest Service on Pohnpei, Federated States of Micronesia. In Micronesia, he has been involved in numerous conservation and development activities. He has essentially become a Pohnpein by choice and by marriage, and has a chiefly title in his village. He is documenting traditional Pohnpeian use of plants and legends about them.

Holmes Rolston III is Professor of Philosophy at Colorado State University. He has been named distinguished lecturer at the 28th Nobel Conference, authorized by the Nobel Foundation, Stockholm, Sweden, October 1992, at Gustavus Adolphus College. He is president of the International Society for Environmental Ethics. He has served as a consultant with two dozen conservation and policy groups. He has been a recipient of NEH and NSF awards. He won the Pennock Award for Distinguished Service at Colorado State University.

Ranil Senanayake, who received his Ph.D. in Ecology from the University of California, Davis, is a senior research scientist at Monash University, Australia; director of the Uva Herbarium in Sri Lanka; and co-director of the NeoSynthesis Research Centre, Sri Lanka. He has worked with the American Museum of Natural History and the California Academy of Sciences as a herpetologist and directs the Zoological Survey of Sri Lanka (amphibia). He currently teaches Applied Forest Ecology in Australia.

Pei Shengji is division head of Mountain Environmental Management and is on the Senior Professional Staff at the International Centre for Integrated Mountain Development based in Kathmandu, Nepal. He was a Professor of Botany at the Kunming Institute of Botany,

Academia Sinica in China. In 1983–84, he was a visiting associate professor at the University of Hawai'i at Manoa and professional associate at the East-West Environment and Policy Institute.

Leslie E. Sponsel received his Ph.D. (1981) in Anthropology from Cornell University. He is an Associate Professor of Anthropology at the University of Hawai'i where he directs the Program in Ecological Anthropology and teaches courses on cultural ecology and human adaptation to tropical forest ecosystems. His early work was carried out among native peoples in Amazonas territory of Venezuela. A current emphasis is on Buddhism and environment, with a focus on Thailand.

Tu Weiming is chair of the Department of East Asian Languages and Civilizations, Harvard University, Cambridge, Massachusetts. He received his Ph.D. in History and East Asian Languages from Harvard University. In 1985, he was a Fulbright Research Scholar in China. He is on the editorial boards of the Harvard Journal of Asiatic Studies, Asian Thought and Society, Philosophy East and West, and Chinese Cultural Quarterly, which is a scholarly journal in Chinese published in Hong Kong. He is currently a member of the Board of Governors of the Institute of East Asian Philosophies in Singapore, a fellow of the American Academy of Arts and Sciences, and president of Contemporary, an intellectual journal published in Taiwan. He was director of the East-West Center's Institute of Culture and Communication in 1990–91.